THE MARKETSPACE:

*Essential Relationships Between the Sending Church,
Marketplace Worker, and Missionary Team*

THE MARKETSPACE:

Essential Relationships Between the Sending Church, Marketplace Worker, and Missionary Team

LARRY E. MCCRARY

To Susan, Megan, and Parker — you have been with me on this journey all the way. I couldn't have worked and traveled the world without you by my side.

To our Upstream Collective team around the world — I could not do any such writing endeavor without your inspiration and encouragement these past ten years. From pastors to missionaries to marketplace workers who have influenced missions in creative ways, thank you!

To my early ideators: Julie Masson, Debbie Stephens, Rodney Calfee, Melissa Fu, Wade Stephens, and Caleb Crider — you all are an inspiration in the way you live your lives.

This book would not be possible without hard work from Amanda May and Bradley Bell with editing, making suggestions, and then editing some more. I appreciate it!

To all my marketspace friends around the globe — your love for Jesus and the way you intentionally live your lives scattered around the world has impacted me, along with so many people. You have truly taken the gospel wherever God has placed you. Thank you!

CONTENTS

Foreword

We needed this book at this time.

In an increasingly complex world, artisans and professionals have a unique opportunity to flourish. With an evolving global marketplace, the challenges of sending qualified people to other cultures are diminishing. Following the prompting of the missionary God, the church has a unique situation before her. She can embrace the opportunity to send out her best to the nations. Now is the time for a growing wave of people to use their skills and careers to advance the gospel.

The Marketspace reads like a conversation with Larry, and those are not to be missed. He graciously gives new ideas to those who are beginning to think about a connection between the gospel and the market. He affirms lay people who are considering joining God on mission among the nations. He grants permission for the church to send out her lay leaders. He encourages the church to embrace and release professionals and artisans as sent ones. And he gives tried, practical advice to traditional missionaries who can work with a growing category of sent ones.

While a tentmaker approach has been around since the time of Paul, this category needs to become a key element of the church's strategy at this time in history. As a practitioner extensively in Europe with experience also in other parts of the globe, Larry has struggled with this reality firsthand. He has found multiple ways forward for all involved. He is uniquely qualified to speak to church leaders and missionaries as peers, and to market professionals as a friend.

This book deserves a reading. *The Marketspace* can serve as a handbook for those who send, as well as for the ones being sent out. My deep thanks go out to my friend, Larry. We needed this book at this time.

Wade Stephens
Co-author of *Tradecraft*
Practitioner of marketplace missions

Missions is dynamic, not static.

The way the church engages the lost world with the gospel is always changing because our world is always changing. For years, phrases like "business as mission" and "business as transformation" have been buzzwords. More than buzzwords, these concepts are viable expressions of getting the gospel to some of the darkest places in the world.

However, local churches and agencies are discovering just how hard it is to do viable and profitable business, while at the same time having fruitful ministry overseas. It takes a special person and a ripe context for this to work well. As a pastor of a local church that values sending, we have been involved in starting businesses overseas, and although some are holding their own, most of them are mediocre at best. We have learned that for us, sending marketspace people to take a job, create a job, study abroad, or connect with some other viable stream in the marketplace is proving to be more successful.

With the global economy and the rise of technology, job markets and educational opportunities are more open than ever in place across the world. The question is, how will the church respond to this opportunity? This book, written by my friend Larry McCrary, does an outstanding job of bringing together the concepts, best practices, and stories of marketplace sending that are beginning to take root in the evangelical missions world. Both agencies and churches alike are taking a harder look at how they can send their people through non-traditional pathways like business and education.

Larry's book is both apologetic in its presentation of why marketplace sending matters and it is also very practical. It provides useful insight and resources about how to send and send well. More than anything, I am excited about this book because it is for the local church. From cover to cover, its intent is to help the local church send its people through creative marketspace pathways in a way that is healthy for the church and for the marketplace missionary.

I am personally thankful for the years Larry has spent learning, developing, and refining these marketplace ideas during his years of service in Madrid and through consulting and training local churches and agencies in different contexts around the world. Larry has both facilitated marketplace sending on the ground and initiated sending from the local church. Churches and agency leaders, as well as prospective marketplace missionaries, will find *The Marketspace* an invaluable resource.

Nathan Garth
Pastor of International Missions
Sojourn Community Church

Despite being from the same state, I first crossed paths with Larry and Susan 13 years ago in Madrid, Spain, when they were the city-wide team leaders for an international missions organization. Like so many who met the McCrarys, I felt an instant affinity with them, thanks to their authenticity, intentionality, and heart for God's mission in the world.

Just a few years later, their example and friendship would accompany me on a radical 180-degree turn in my career: leaving the safety of the sending agency in favor of searching for a job in the local marketplace in Europe.

The content presented in *The Marketspace* brings back memories of long, late-night conversations Larry, Susan, and I had during my transition into the labor market overseas. Even though this book didn't exist as such, the McCrarys helped me explore the biblical concepts presented here. God used their experience and advice to propel me toward a long-term career abroad, which allows me to incarnate the love of Christ on a deeper level among a people I adore.

This guide will be a tremendous resource for the increasing number of Christ-followers like me who consider careers abroad as part of the Great Commission. This expression of missions is not just legitimized but is held up as an example in Scripture; yet it is often overlooked in many Western cultures. The good news is that now, everyone from students to business travelers to expatriated professionals are taking the call to "go therefore" seriously. *The Marketspace* is the perfect preparation material for these individuals.

The Marketspace also has huge implications for the churches who love and want to support the overseas, on-mission professional. In this type of non-traditional missions partnership, neither the sending church nor the "sent one" can afford to be passive. This book provides active, creative, yet practical steps both parties can take in response to what God is doing all over the world. My desire is also that it raises awareness among churches of the need to encourage, commission, train, and support these non-traditional missionaries.

I hope you find the concepts in this book to be as challenging and enriching as I have. Many blessings as you explore your place in the marketspace.

Melissa Fu

PREFACE: SECOND-CLASS MISSIONARIES?

There has been an awakening in the mission world.

More and more marketplace people are willing to take their jobs overseas or create jobs, working abroad with intentionality. More and more mission sending agencies are desiring a way to see this model of marketspace sending thrive.

But we have a major challenge. For the past 25 years, I have served as an elder, church planter, pastor, and missionary, both overseas and in the United States, I am in between a rock and a hard place. I'm caught between both worlds: the world of the marketspace missionary and the pastor's world. So when I tell you about the potential problem, consider me a part of it.

Both pastors and missionaries can be part of the problem. Quite frankly, pastors often do not see marketspace ministry as a viable expression of mission. We can be so glued to the standard archetype of professional and vocational missionaries that we miss the bigger picture of God releasing hundreds of thousands of believers all over the world. These men and women are salt and light, wherever they are placed.

Pastors are not quite sure what to do with this type of worker that does not need financial support. How can we assess them to see if they are good cross-cultural candidates? How can we send them if they aren't going through traditional sending agencies? How do we remember to pray for them if they do not have prayer cards? How do we provide accountability for them if they are not part of an official team? How can we shepherd these people well? Often, we ask, "Isn't that what the mission organization does?"

We also have the danger of the full-time missionary teams not knowing how to receive this type of worker. It is unconventional, right? They do not have the organizational ties that full-time missionaries have. We cannot tell them what to do. They are part time, so how can they really be part of a team? After all, they are not involved in the "main thing," the making of disciples, all of the time. Quite frankly, we often treat them as second-class missionaries — forgetting that the space in which they live and work overseas provides them with incredible access to the very people we are trying to engage.

This book was intended to address these concerns, as well as to introduce the five essential components of global marketplace ministry. Whether you are a pastor, missions organizational leader, missionary, or are considering taking your job overseas, you will find answers to your questions about where and how you can serve.

It may be helpful to think of this with the following diagram. It takes all four all of these spheres working together.

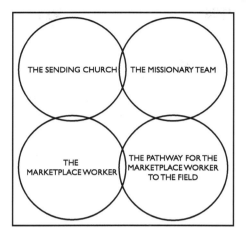

Circle one represents missionary teams praying for and asking for alternative pathways people to come alongside and serve on their teams in specific roles and responsibilities.

In many cases, I see missionary organizations trying to mobilize individuals to consider such pathways. While I do not see this as inherently wrong, I would prefer to see sending churches (that see this as a viable pathway) mobilizing their church, and thus having these people ready and willing to take these new pathways. I think the church is in a better and more sustainable position to mobilize, rather than waiting for the individual to awaken and take the initiative to ask the church for support. It can work both ways, but my preference is to see the church take the lead in these efforts, just as often as they cast vision for members to go to the nations as vocational missionaries. What if the church actively tries to mobilize both types of workers? Not to mention, it may be a more sustainable way to send out church-based teams.

I envision the sending church (circle two) mobilizing and equipping people in their church to take these alternative pathway approaches.

I see men and women coming from these churches and getting the proper training and preparation (circle three) to work alongside missionary teams and choosing the appropriate pathway for them (circle four).

My hope is for you to find your place on this journey in marketspace ministry. Whether you are a seasoned pastor, a veteran missionary, or someone weighing the options of relocating overseas, your role is equally valuable in God's sight.

INTRODUCTION: AN "AHA!" MOMENT

There was a formula for creating good worship events, and I had it down. Loud music, engaging video clips or drama sketches, excellent preaching, quality childcare, a cool website, flashy signs, and good coffee — these were the keys to catching the interest of church seekers. My wife, Susan, and I had begun planting churches in the northern suburbs of Atlanta and then in Dallas/Fort Worth. If I'm honest, we were good at church planting — at least, that's what we thought.

In many ways, I became as much of an event planner as I did a church planter. Even though we knew all the working parts, putting them together still took time. Sunday mercilessly came around every seven days, so Monday morning brought the arduous task of evaluating, streamlining, and planning for the next worship service. We were really good at creating an experience, an exceptional church service. The problem was that we had become proficient at the wrong thing.

Unfortunately, all my event planning had gotten in the way of the core of the Great Commission: making disciples that make disciples to the nations. There was no doubt in our minds: top-notch services didn't necessarily equal making disciples. Do not get me wrong: we valued the gathering of the saints in worship, Bible teaching, and prayer. However, the things that seemed to be often emphasized, like good coffee, comfy chairs, and casual greeting times to avoid awkwardness (well, most of it) weren't teaching people to obey everything Jesus commanded. In fact, doing all those things really well kept us from accomplishing the one thing we were explicitly sent to do. We weren't training followers of Jesus, much less disciples who discipled others with the entire world in mind.

That isn't to say we weren't seeing people come to Christ, or that our efforts were in vain. That's not true at all. We served a gracious God who multiplied our feeble efforts. But if I had a mulligan, just one do-over, I would go back and change our focus. From the very beginning, I would implant within the hearts and minds of every church member the same desire that rests in the heart and mind of God: people from every nation, tribe, people, and language worshiping around his throne.

It had finally begun making sense to me while at one of my last church plants in the States in the 90s. My wife and I together began to ask the question, "How can we start making disciples who have the nations in mind?"

Let me take a moment here to offer some clarity. I am not writing any of this to rail against churches or methods or excellence or any of the things listed above. Good teaching is a good thing, for adults and children. Finding people with the potential to lead the local church in worship, equipping them to use those gifts, and then setting them free to do so — even really loudly, is a good thing. Good coffee, well, that's a great thing! My point is not to say that those things in themselves are not good. Yet if they detract from the best thing — declaring the gospel in word and deed, growing people in the image of Christ, and sending them as kingdom representatives both locally and globally — then, yeah, I'll rail against them. I know what it's like to settle for less than God's best, and I don't want anyone to repeat my mistakes.

After I completed my seminary education, I served at a large church in Chattanooga, Tennessee. Susan and I loved that church and learned so much about ministry while we were there. We really believe God used us in some very special ways, far beyond what we had imagined. For whatever reason, we were able to relate well with young business professionals who were disconnected from the church. As I look back now, I am convinced God gave us valuable experience and empowered us with those in the marketplace to prepare our hearts and minds for the future. It was a future we did not expect in the least.

One evening, Susan and I were participating in a missions conference. She is a violinist and accompanied the musicians that evening. I was sitting in my normal spot, the very back. By the end of the service, however, we found ourselves together in an unexpected place. We met at the altar, each sensing that God was leading us into church planting and global missions. Neither of us knew the other would be there, nor that God was speaking the same thing in our hearts simultaneously. Maybe we shouldn't have been so surprised that God would compel us that way. However, before that night, missions hadn't even been a blip on our radar.

"Go therefore and make disciples of all nations, baptizing them in the name of the Father and of the Son and of the Holy Spirit, teaching them to observe all that I have commanded you. And behold, I am with you always, to the end of the age" (Matthew 28:19-20). If you're reading this book, you are likely familiar with this passage we call the Great Commission. You've heard it taught in your local church and at missions conferences and on podcasts, and you've seen it on coffee mugs, websites, and headlining every piece of missions literature, ever. Yeah, me too. I memorized the passage as a kid and studied it in seminary and preached it in the churches I was planting.

So, how could the Great Commission have possibly caused us problems?

Susan and I were committed to going somewhere, though we weren't really sure where we might end up. We had experienced an undeniable call to go together. Meeting each other at the altar of a missions conference was our very own burning bush ... an "aha!" moment for each of us. We believed God had sent us to Atlanta and Dallas. But sent us for what? To what end?

In 2001, we moved to Madrid, Spain. Viva España!

It wasn't that we felt forced to move overseas in order to make global disciples. In fact, the term "global disciple" is actually a redundancy. The word "disciple" alone, when used in the Christian context, carries with it the full weight of God's desire to fill the earth with the knowledge of his glory as waters cover the sea, including the integral part his people play in achieving it. Every disciple of Jesus should by nature have a global outlook.

For us, that meant setting off for Spain with our two young children in tow. We worked with an organization called the IMB (International Mission Board), and I soon became a strategist overseeing engagement with urban professionals. We were so grateful for that first church that had long ago given us the opportunity to work among young business professionals — and to the God who had foreseen that we would need such a skill set. In so many ways, it was my dream job.

We immediately got to work — and there was a lot to do. For starters, we had to:
- master a different language
- understand a new culture
- plant the gospel among the people
- forge relationships among professionals

And so much more.

It was going to be an uphill climb, but thankfully I had a strategy. I was certain I could build a team that would totally change the landscape of Christianity in Madrid. I would recruit high-performance missionaries who would learn the language and culture together, pray and worship together, and connect with young urban professionals in order to make influential disciples across the city. Flawless plan. You know, except for the huge, glaring flaws.

We were limited in several important areas. Needless to say, my dream was short-lived. I bitterly realized I was not going to be able to do this on my own, nor alongside the team we assembled. Our teammates were amazing, but we ran into several factors that slowed or, in some cases, halted our work completely.

LIMITED NUMBER OF WORKERS

There was no way I could build a fully-funded missionary team that was large enough to accomplish my goals. Eventually, I realized we shouldn't have even tried. Though we did need a few full-time vocational Christian workers, at the end of the day, a few were more than enough. Limits on this resource forced us to partner with local, national marketspace workers who loved Jesus, followed Him daily, and were willing to live with gospel-focused intentionality. They provided their own resources simply because they worked full-time. Obviously, they had less time for planning, strategizing, and goal setting, due to their daytime jobs, but they quickly became valuable members of our team for a number of reasons that we will examine soon.

LIMITED ACCESS TO THE PEOPLE

At first, my entire team was full-time Christian workers. Our days were filled with meetings, language study, and the daily grind of cultural transition. Even though we lived in strategic parts of the city, we simply did not work alongside the business people we were trying to engage with the gospel. At best, we were teetering on the edge of cultural acceptance. Sure, we could strike up conversations with strangers, but those opportunities were sorely lacking when it came to the people we were strategically trying to reach.

Think about it: many people spend the majority of their adult lives inside the workplace — and that was the one place to which our team did not have open access. We didn't have jobs that gave us significant and prolonged reasons to be in their office buildings and factories and stores. Furthermore, we found out that in our European context it was a regular practice to hang out with co-workers outside the office. So, for our purposes, the significance of connecting in the marketspace wasn't just important — it was imperative.

LIMITED CREDIBILITY

We had very little credibility in the marketspace. Most full-time Christian workers are theologically trained and often have little business experience. That's my story, too. I'm not ashamed of my seminary education nor ministry experience. It's simply the reality for much of my generation of professional Christian workers.

However, the challenge for our team was that business people were our specific people group. Many of our team-mates often found themselves at a loss as to how to even begin a conversation with people whose entire existence revolved around their profession, along with their unique subculture and jargon. Simply put, we were out of place in the marketspace.

Of course, God's power is always made perfect in our weakness, and he caused our fumbling attempts to bear a little fruit. Yet Jesus is clear, his will is that we bear much fruit (John 15:8). Engaging fruitfully in the marketspace required navigating the language and culture of the marketspace. It demanded the experience and credibility we didn't have.

The things our team was discovering then have been reaffirmed over and over to me in the years since. Having met many Christian marketspace workers around the world, it amazes me how regularly they are invited to homes, family gatherings, and other social settings after hours. A place within the market not only secured access to people during work hours, but a place within the social order as well.

After about a year in Spain, I realized I had made several friends from all over the world who happened to live in Madrid. They were all business people, working jobs in the marketspace. Most of them had been transferred by international companies and found themselves living in Madrid. They loved Jesus and wanted to tell others about him; they wanted to live as salt and light. They were in the marketspace and knew how to relate to other workers there, so they had access and credibility in places I could not reach. They wanted to live on mission, yet they did not know where to start.

So I took advantage of the long Spanish lunch hour, and we started our journey toward engaging their workmates with the gospel. Each of us was involved in a church, so our time together was not meant to be that. We prayed for one another, encouraged one another, held each other accountable, and addressed issues about settling our families into a new culture. In fact, we began to get our families together to share meals and hang out. Our main purpose, however, was to wrestle with how they could leverage their careers for the sake of the gospel. We talked about building relationships with co-workers that would offer opportunities to share the good news of Jesus with them.

I realized very quickly that these men and women had greater access than I did to the very people I was sent there to engage. They worked together on a daily basis, so they had the opportunity to go to coffee or share a meal with them. They had a reason to get their families together. Sadly, that was just not true for me — at least, not to the extent of my friends. They enjoyed a credibility among the local workforce that I simply did not. We often talk about taking the gospel wherever you live, work, and play. I could only function with credibility where I lived and played. I didn't have a work space that made sense to the people we were trying to engage.

At the end of the day, I worked for a non-profit organization that wanted to plant the gospel among the people in the city. The average person on the street could not comprehend why in the world my family and I were in Spain. We did not work in the same way they did. Our schedules were not the same. Our priorities were not the same. Many of our neighbors asked why we were even there. They could not see a reason for our presence in their city. On the other hand, my friends who worked in the marketplace instantly connected with locals because they were involved in business together. They kept the same hours. They ran in the same social circles. Their reasons for being there were immediately obvious.

I soon realized that this group of men and women were just as legitimately on mission as I was. They wouldn't necessarily use that moniker, but they were missionaries nonetheless. **And the best part was that they all had a viable pathway to mission.** In fact, they really had far better access to the people I was there to reach than I did. Though I was the only one who was paid to do ministry and the only one who bore the title "missionary," they were far from second-class witnesses. They were doing what Christ followers are meant to do and have always been doing. In the words of Mike Barnett, the late Dean of Intercultural Studies at Columbia International University, said, "We are not innovators. God has been using businessmen and women for centuries to take the gospel to the nations."

I think there are five essential components that we must keep in mind as we encourage people who are already in this "marketspace ministry:"

- The marketspace worker needs the blessing of a sending church
- The marketspace worker needs a legitimate reason to be there
- The marketspace worker, the sending church, and the missionary team need to be trained and equipped for their special roles
- The marketspace worker needs a viable community to thrive in
- The marketspace worker needs to seize opportunities with a strategic focus

This book will unravel these five components. We will look at how the church can bless and empower nontraditional missionaries, which pathways believers can travel in order to provide a legitimate reason for their stay, and so much more. These components will benefit Christians already in the marketspace, as well as those who send them.

PART ONE:
THE BLESSING OF A SENDING CHURCH

We have created a chasm between the clergy and the lay person. We have taken that same idea again in missions. There are broad categories, such as full-time missionaries, tentmakers, short-term workers, etc. In many missions organizations, you even have subcategories of distinction in serving (short-term workers, mid-term workers, two-year program after college, two-year program after retirement, long-term career, etc). The church needs to help marketspace workers who move overseas feel validated in their missionary efforts.

People who are on the field now but not "sent" by an agency share the same desire. They long to feel like they are being "sent" by their church. Most churches simply view them as professionals who live overseas and are away from their church. What if the church blessed these people like they do full-time missionaries sent by agencies? What if they laid hands on them and prayed for them and gave them every bit the validation of being sent as we do the professional missionaries?

Think about how it feels to be blessed. Think about the

empowerment you feel when someone of credibility affirms you and sends you. For the vast majority of people, this blessing serves as incredible motivation to do the work.

Obviously, there are differences that have to be addressed in distinguishing between the two types of mission efforts. But the longer I am in the professional missionary category, the more I am convinced it needs to be radically changed and this new way to become the standard. We spend so much of our time overseas in meetings, doing administrative tasks, keeping up with policy, raising support, and the list can go on and on. Most of these things have to be done. I am not arguing that. But what if, by working legitimate jobs overseas, we are able to spend the bulk of our time interacting with nationals and entering into their world in our jobs?

At the end of the day, as missionaries, we want to be deep into the ethno-linguistic core of the people — but often our own organization or professional pathway can become the very thing that keeps us from that.

After spending two years as vocational missionaries in Africa, Stephen and Amy* (names have been changed) found themselves in France as newlyweds. He was starting school, and she was on the hunt for job opportunities in France. This may sound like the beginning of a romantic European lifestyle for a young couple, but reality couldn't have been further from the truth. Amy spent almost the entire first year and a half looking for work. It was a vicious cycle. She needed a work permit to apply for a job. She couldn't get a work permit if she didn't have a job. Their first few years were not what you would envision when you think of an American couple living in France. To top it off, they were living among a people who are somewhat closed to new relationships with outsiders.

To sum things up, life in France was hard. They had hardly any money, friends, or support from a church back home. Sure, family and friends prayed for them and encouraged them as best they could, but they felt very alone most of the time. Even when Amy was able to secure a job, there was still a sense that their existence in France was merely that — an existence. Eventually, a church in Oklahoma decided to "adopt" them. This church decided that what Amy and Stephen were doing in France (living among the locals, working and studying in the marketplace) was a really great and valid way to live life. A relationship was formed, and the couple was encouraged that they were not alone in this quest to live a gospel-saturated life in France.

The Oklahoma church kept in communication with Stephen and Amy via email and Skype, and they even sent a few care packages. It meant the world to a young couple living alone, without the support of fellow Christ followers. It was also a constant reminder that although God sent them to France for school, he had plans to use them for his glory during their time there.

Active involvement and support from your home church is vital to your time overseas. It's important to have a group of people who will regularly pray for your ministry while also praying for your own spiritual growth. We understand that not everyone leaves for the marketspace with the support of a sending church. I am sort of promoting an ideal. If you do not have that type of church, hang in there or tell them to contact me. I'm serious.

Another important thing to consider is the strategy of the sending church. I work with a lot of churches who are scaling down the number of partnerships overseas in order to zero in on just a few, depending on the size of the church. These churches are taking a comprehensive look at how to truly engage and invest in a city. They are not simply taking short-term trips overseas; they are working a strategy for a particular city. They are:

- praying for that city, place, or people as a church
- sending strategic short-term teams to help on the ground to support or to establish some relationships
- inspiring college students to study abroad in those areas
- encouraging people who have retired to spend strategic time there
- finding out if any of their business people work in those countries
- motivating marketspace workers to look for ways to start companies there or simply get transferred there

Recently, I was in a midwestern city at a church. We had a gathering of young adults who were interested in working overseas on purpose. As we were talking, a very cool conversation took place. A young man was telling how he and his wife wanted to do this, and that he had just had a conversation with his employer today about the possibilities of transferring to a job in Asia. As he was telling this story and describing the city, the pastor of the church had the strangest look on his face. He blurted out, "Did you know our church just started a strategic partnership in that city?" WOW. It is so encouraging to know that God is eager to make connections between churches and marketplace workers.

I was part of a group that wrote the book *Tradecraft: For the Church on Mission*. In it, we refer to a diagram that displays our need for churches to think of Spirit-led missions in every aspect of sending. We do not want to see church members simply go with a missions organization and their church not join in. We do not want to see business people take a transfer without the church feeling included. Instead, we want to see the church take a holistic approach to their strategy.

THE PATHS TO MISSION

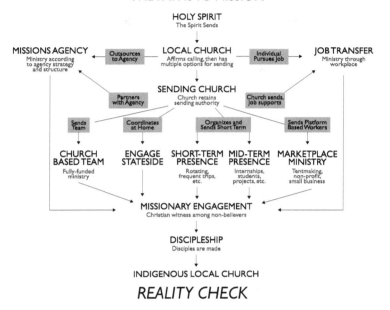

REALITY CHECK

Marketspace workers make up the majority of every church's membership. Yet, the reality is there is only a small percentage who usually take part in God's mission. They are the ones who are trained, sent, and expected to engage in missions, because they are the "professionals." That leaves the vast majority of the missionary force in our churches untrained, unsent, and unengaged. But

THE VAST MAJORITY OF THE MISSIONARY FORCE IN OUR CHURCHES ARE UNTRAINED, UNSENT, AND UNENGAGED.

the Great Commission does not belong only to the full-time ordained Christian workers. The mission is the responsibility of every follower of Christ.

If we believe that to be true, then it must affect our churches. It must affect who and how we equip and send. It means that we must depend more on the "professionals" to act as equippers, as Ephesians 4 prescribes, and release the rest of the missionary force as fully-trained missionaries in their own neighborhoods and into the nations. We need to start preparing our marketspace people (which includes most of the church) to be able to take the gospel wherever they are, in whatever profession they are in, to their neighbors and to the nations. Part of the training we need to prioritize is to correct the misunderstanding that all missionary engagement is sequential. That is how we have most often understood Acts 1:8, as a progression:

Step 1: Gospel to Jerusalem
Step 2: Gospel to Judea
Step 3: Gospel to Samaria
Step 4: Gospel to the ends of the earth

We often think and teach that the church's mission is a step-by-step sequence of events. We must reach our city first. Then we can work on our state. After that, the nation. And finally, the world. There are a few problems with that thought process.

First, it is not the model presented by the early church.

The explosion of the church in the first century was certainly centrifugal, but not necessarily sequential. The church in Jerusalem was still undergoing birth pangs as the gospel moved outward into the surrounding areas toward the ends of the earth.

Second, such a process simply doesn't make good practical sense. If we wait until our home turf is "reached," we can rest assured that most of our churches won't ever venture outside of our cities. There's also no biblical prescription for defining what it means for a particular area to be "reached." How would we even know when it is time to step out of one area into the next?

Third, if we only focus on one area at a time, we miss the opportunity for one to inform and serve the other. There is a long-held understanding among churches that participation in some sort of missions opportunity outside of your home culture is the best motivator for local involvement within your home culture. And an active church at home often produces people who are passionate, gifted, and equipped for global missions as well. They belong together.

This sequential view also denies people, who may be both gifted and passionate for global mission, the opportunity to engage meaningfully where they could make a great difference.

There is another secondary result of this thinking that is just as — if not more — dangerous than the previously mentioned problems. **It is an identity problem.** If preference is given to one part of the Great Commission over the other, it can very easily cause a divergence in identity. Those who go to certain places and/or do certain things take on a different identity than the remainder of their Christian counterparts. If most of the church is focused only at home, then it is easy to see how those who are sent to the ends of the earth become highly revered. History proves that just such a thing has happened, and the church has elevated the call and "profession" of missionary to a place of prominence.

With the the rise of the "professional missionary" class come even greater problems. First, the expectations placed on those who are sent out as professional missionaries can be unbearable. The weight of the mission sits firmly on the shoulders of the few, which was never intended. The mission of the church belongs to the whole church. The clergy/laity divide that is evident in our stateside churches often places the work and ministry of the local church on the shoulders of the pastor. The missionary/non-missionary divide takes that separation one step further — one more degree from everyday Christian to believer fully engaged in God's global mission. The identity of the Christian is affected, shifting from a singular identity as witness and ambassador to either a missionary or an everyday Christian. One of those is far more highly revered, resulting in the diminution of the other's role in God's mission.

Inherent identity problems aside, we face another, more practical issue in missions, in that the nations have moved in next door. It was once true that engaging people of a different culture meant picking up your life and moving where they were. That is increasingly not the case any longer. The nations have come to us as Western populations have grown increasingly diverse. They are our neighbors. Take a quick look around and you'll find:

Somalis in Columbus, Ohio
Turks in Dayton, Illinois
Kurds in Nashville, Tennessee
The world in New York, Houston, Los Angeles,
Seattle, Vancouver, Toronto

If we are going to faithfully share the gospel among these groups of people, we must rethink our methods for doing so. Do we only send full-time Christian workers to engage other cultures with the gospel? Or do we equip the business people, the teachers, the artists, the moms, and the dads to be involved in more than just functions of the Sunday service and involve them in the Great Commission wherever they live, work, and play? Do we mobilize the entire church in the mission for the sake of the gospel and the good of those who've not heard it — even our nextdoor neighbors? My contention is to stop

> IF WE ARE GOING TO FAITHFULLY SHARE THE GOSPEL AMONG THESE GROUPS OF PEOPLE, WE MUST RETHINK OUR METHODS FOR DOING SO.

limiting our equipping and sending; stop reserving it only for the minority of people that can live overseas as full-time Christian workers via a missions organization.

THE CHALLENGE

Somehow, intentionally or not, many American Christians were taught that being a professional missionary is a higher calling — the best and most appropriate way to respond to a call to missions. In some cases, we've been taught it is the only way to respond to such a call. But, as you've already guessed, I propose that being a full-time Christian worker is not the only way to be an effective missionary overseas. Others who subscribe to a more traditional methodology disagree, so this is a fairly contentious conversation in the current missions arena. However, if we are going to equip and release a missionary force, the likes of which modern missions has not seen, we must address it.

FRONT-LINE MISSION IS THE RIGHT AND RESPONSIBILITY OF EVERY BELIEVER.

We have to begin to break down the missionary/non-missionary divide and help all people realize their distinct place in the mission of God. All believers must realize that mission is their identity. It is not an add-on or a special role reserved for a particular few. Front-line mission is the right and responsibility of every believer.

Please, don't miss that. Let me speak directly to you, business person, plumber, painter, musician, pilot, truck driver: you are an ambassador. You are a representative of Christ in all that you do. That is your identity.

Pastors, every person in your churches is there as an ambassador of Christ, and you are there to equip them for the work of ministry, whether locally or somewhere around the globe. Encourage every single believer in your congregations to walk into his or her identity. Equip your people for the mission. I believe this may be the greatest challenge we face in our churches. Leveling the playing field — so every believer has the opportunity to participate in missions — requires a great deal of change. I fear that many of our churches will not be able to stomach the extent of cultural shift needed to accomplish it. However, if we can, we have the opportunity to grow our missionary force exponentially.

I must admit that even as I write these ideas, I may not be the right man to implement them. I am not a businessman, and I never have been. I have three seminary degrees, including a doctorate, and I am an ordained pastor. I have lived outside my country of origin as a professional missionary in the employ of a large missions organization. I have been an employee of said organization for 15 years, before which I was a pastor and church planter in the States.

Now for my business credentials. When I was 15, I worked in the warehouse of a carpet company. I was rarely allowed to go out front and interact with customers. Between the ages of 16 and 19, I worked for a paint company, beginning in the warehouse and working my way to inside sales. Along the way, I also worked for my father, who owned his own business, operated my own small landscaping business, and worked in a manufacturing plant for a short time. I learned a strong work ethic during these years, including how to keep commitments, deliver a quality product or service on time, and treat people with respect.

Apart from that, though, my secular employment history is pretty scant. So, if you are a business person reading these words, you may find yourself hesitating to believe I have the expertise to talk about business as mission. The thing is, from a business standpoint, you're probably right. I'm not the guy to help you develop your business plan and put it into action. I'm not the guy to help you understand international business laws or secure work visas or answer your tax questions. That's not who I am, and it's not the reason I'm writing. Obviously, I believe that people like me are still good and necessary within the missionary enterprise. I simply want to say, "So are you."

I don't envision you walking away from these ideas with a complete plan in hand to start a business overseas. I merely want you to understand that God can use you in that way for the sake of his mission. You do not have to quit your day job or give up your dream of being a veterinarian or a violinist or a business owner. God can use those things for his glory in your hometown or around the world.

For those of you who are in full-time Christian ministry like myself and reading these words, it is my prayer that you will join me in leading the charge to change the church's understanding of missionary involvement. Join me in encouraging believers to seek the Lord in regard to his or her own role in the mission. **Let's join together to alleviate the bottleneck and open wide the gates for the missionary involvement of every believer.**

It will take all of us. Pastors, seminary professors, missionary organization leaders: let's recognize and trumpet the truth that the marketspace around the globe is fertile ground for expression of the Great Commission.

The people who can engage others in the marketspace are the people who are passionate for the marketspace, and we need to prepare and encourage them to go. You may not be able count them in your missionary list or include them on your church's website. They may not wear your mission organization's logo on their shirt, but they count. They can accomplish through their natural course of work and daily rhythms things that we full-time missionaries may not be able to accomplish through years of service, if ever.

Recently, I was having a conversation with a friend who served effectively with a missions organization in Europe. He transitioned from being a full-time Christian worker to a marketspace worker. His reasoning for doing so really stuck with me. He said, "I am completely sold on encouraging and empowering this kind of 'non-missionary missionary'

— marketspace professionals who are fulfilling their call to missions through their careers and choose to live overseas on purpose." Yes. A thousand times, yes!

THE OPPORTUNITY

With that said, we stand on the precipice of incredible opportunity. It is beyond time for us to recognize both the need for and the value of non-traditional missionaries through marketspace work. In many circles, particularly in large global cities, the consensus is that the best way to be a missionary is NOT to be a "missionary," at least not in the traditional sense. As I mentioned earlier, my family and co-workers in Europe found that the most effective way to impact our neighbors is by entering the culture as "one of the gang." And the most effective way to accomplish that is through having a place in the market.

That's where having a normal job comes in. It is time to elevate and validate the calling of these marketspace missionaries who take seriously the responsibility to live out their faith incarnationally overseas. It is time for the local church to equip and send the whole of the available missionary force, sending out its best and brightest to live and work abroad; getting more personally

IT IS TIME TO ELEVATE AND VALIDATE THE CALLING OF THESE MARKETSPACE MISSIONARIES.

involved in God's mission through prayer; being present on the field both short and long-term; and learning how to take good care of their newly-commissioned business executives, students, waiters, graphic designers ... you get the picture.

We envision a community for Christ–following expatriates to live out their lives with intentionality — to be salt and light where they live, work, and play around the world. Hear Jesus' words: "You are the salt of the earth, but if salt has lost its taste, how shall its saltiness be restored? It is no longer good for anything except to be thrown out and trampled under people's feet. You are the light of the world. A city set on a hill cannot be hidden. Nor do people light a lamp and put it under a basket, but on a stand, and it gives light to all in the house. In the same way, let your light shine before others, so that they may see your good works and give glory to your father who is in heaven" (Matthew 5:13-16). This is meant for every Christ follower, not just missionaries.

Melissa worked for a traditional missions organization for about a year. She had a very successful term, but recognized that it was hard to explain what she did with her university-student friends. She just had a real burden to live and work as a regular person, not worry about raising support, and not be connected to a missions organization. She felt this would give her stronger credibility with the group she was trying to engage. Sure enough, she was able to land a job, after several months and much hard work. Melissa has now been there for eight or nine years working at a regular job in Spain, and she is very involved with her church. It is especially strategic about trying to reach Spaniards, and she is leading a Spanish Bible study on a weekly basis. She has made a real impact in the marketspace.

This is true for all Christ-followers. We are meant to illuminate the glory of Christ wherever we are, and we have the opportunity to engage people groups around the world for just that purpose through the marketspace.

WHEREVER WE ARE

Speaking to his disciples just before he ascended into heaven, Jesus said, "You will be my witnesses in Jerusalem and in all Judea and Samaria, and to the end of the earth" (Acts 1:8). The word "witness" Jesus used is as much about your identity as a Christ follower as it is an action. We are meant to "witness" to others, which is an activity. But we all are also "witnesses," which is an identity based on the fact that we have seen and experienced something that must be shared. God changed us — he has saved and redeemed us through the redemptive activity of Christ on the cross. We, then, are people whose identity is defined by that role. It is who we are. **We are salt and light to a world in need of the gospel.** Wherever we are and whatever we do, we are meant to be witnesses.

Back to the team I led in Madrid. Our team's journey was not only depicted in the experience of global professionals, it was seemingly prescribed by the Bible. In Acts 17, for example, Paul utilized the marketspace as a strategic part of his mission: "Now while Paul was waiting for them at Athens, his spirit was provoked within him as he saw that the city was full of idols. So he reasoned in the synagogue with the Jews and the devout persons, and in the marketplace every day with those who happened to be there. Some of the Epicurean and Stoic philosophers also conversed with him" (Acts 17:16-18).

The Spirit had led Paul on quite a journey prior to this point, and his time in Athens would prove to be no less spectacular. As soon as he entered the city, he was immediately troubled. He made his way through the city and up to the temple of Athena, situated on the city's highest point. There he began to notice the countless idols for honoring and worshiping various gods. His spirit, the Scriptures say, was provoked within him. He was keenly aware of the spiritual blindness, and he grieved along with the Holy Spirit. Thus, Paul was driven to action, reasoning with all of those around him concerning what he saw in the city. There are a number of things we could consider regarding this passage, but I'd like to point out three distinct spaces in which Paul engaged the Athenians with the gospel:

THE RELIGIOUS SPACE

It was quite a normal occurrence for Paul to engage the Jews on their own turf. Having been an exemplary and zealous Jew himself, he understood their beliefs and practices. More importantly, he recognized that Christ was indeed the one for whom they were all waiting. So he consistently engaged them in their place of prayer and sacrifice. In Acts 16, we read of Paul's experience in Philippi: "[A]nd from there to Philippi, which is a leading city of the district of Macedonia and a Roman colony. We remained in this city some days. And on the Sabbath day we went outside the gate to the riverside, where we supposed there was a place of prayer, and we sat down and spoke to the women who had come together" (16:12-13).

Paul was simply contextualizing, meeting people where they were and communicating the gospel in ways they could understand. As he spoke with the women about the finished work of Christ, one of them, Lydia, believed. She and her family were baptized, and she invited Paul and Silas to stay in her home, where a church was eventually planted.

In Acts 17, Paul employed the same practice. He went to the synagogue and reasoned among the Jews gathered there to worship. Utilizing his knowledge of the law and experience as a Pharisee, he was able to proclaim the good news with credibility. He knew the space. He knew how to exist there. Thus, he was able to preach the good news there.

THE STORY SPACE

Not only did Paul engage the Athenians within their religious context, he also made his way into their social circles. He went to the place where people loved to hang out and discuss the meaning of life. That was where you could find the Stoic and Epicurean philosophers. They loved being on the cutting edge of new thought, and Paul knew it. As he discussed the lordship of Christ and his resurrection, it was news indeed, and irresistible to the debating, high-minded philosophers.

You've seen this situation before, right? Every small town has a Hardee's or McDonald's where old men hang out in the morning to talk. They discuss life and love and loss and fishing and baseball and whatever else might be the flavor of the day. They are usually not a quiet bunch, so now and again some outsider may walk by and throw an idea in the mix. But no one sits down unless they are invited to do so.

In Madrid, it is Cafe Gijon, where the men gather and talk about literature, philosophy, or some other topic that draws their attention as they sip thoughtfully on their cafe con leche. In Athens, talkers convened in the Areopagus. In fact, the Areopagus was actually an official gathering place where legal cases were heard. In this instance, however, they invited Paul there to talk about their gods, and this new God whom he was referencing. Paul was able to communicate the gospel strategically in another "space" of the city.

THE MARKETSPACE

The third place Paul connected was the marketspace. He was able to do so because he was familiar with it. In fact, you could say he belonged there.

This passage is a narrow window into Paul's daily life. We discover how he made his living: "After this, Paul left Athens and went to Corinth. And he found a Jew named Aquila, a native of Pontus, recently come from Italy with his wife Priscilla, because Claudius had commanded all the Jews to leave Rome. And he went to see them, and because he was of the same trade he stayed with them and worked, for they were tentmakers by trade. And he reasoned in the synagogue every Sabbath, and tried to persuade Jews and Greeks" (Acts 18:1-4).

See it there? Evidently, Paul had been a tentmaker by trade. He was a tentmaker — not in the figurative way we use the term in missions now, but literally. Paul made and sold tents. That means that at some point, he supported himself in the mission work he was doing by way of a profitable trade. I think we can assume he had learned his trade along the way and practiced it at some point as his means of support. When Paul arrived in Corinth, he connected with Aquila and Priscilla, and was able to stay with them and use his skill set.

When people practice a trade, they share common ground with others who do the same. They have a common affinity. They speak the same language. In Paul's case, he could identify with others who worked with their hands and depended on the profits from selling their goods to put food on the table. People readily identified with his theological treatises. They expected him to communicate deep theological truths to the churches with whom he partnered.

Can you imagine his conversations in the marketspace, though? He talked with others, like Priscilla and Aquila, who worked with their hands. "What kind of fabric are you using in your tents?" he might have asked of someone selling tents close by in the marketplace. "The purple color is fit for a king. In fact, let me tell you of my king for whom I am making this tent. He owned nothing so fancy..."

Paul could connect with others in the marketspace because he shared their experiences. He understood a hard day's work, a sweaty brow, and a livelihood based on his ability to create a desirable product. He knew how to trade and sell his goods, and he invariably knew the struggles of a profitable market versus a weak one. His work gave him credibility and entry into a tribe which otherwise may not have accepted him.

LIVING ON MISSION

It is estimated that today there are more than 8.7 million U.S. citizens who live abroad.[1] For the sake of ease, let's assume a conservative estimate that roughly 10% of those expatriates are Christ followers. That would mean there are more than 800,000 believers who are in the worldwide marketspace. This is a staggering number, especially when compared to the relatively meager numbers of full-time Christian missionaries that missions organizations

[1] The Association of Americans Resident Overseas. "8.7M Americans Abroad." AARO.org. 2016.

are able to fund.

What if those 800,000 people lived out their lives strategically as God's people on mission?

What if they built relationships with people from their new host countries — relationships with people in the marketspace — to which full-time Christian missionaries may not have access?

What if they were trained and equipped to take advantage of the opportunities to share the gospel in natural settings as global workers?

What if they believed they were there for God's glory and to make disciples?

What if they were able to start Bible study groups with those new believers that eventually led to new churches?

I can tell you from personal experience that many expatriate believers are doing exactly that. **They are not missionaries in the traditional sense of being full-time paid Christian workers, but they are living their lives on mission.** They are living out the Great Commission through the marketspace, and they are seeing results as their friends and co-workers come to faith in Christ.

Imagine the impact of infusing the existing missionary workforce with 800,000 missionaries who have already rooted themselves in community, a purpose for being there, a sustainable means of income, and have natural access to people in desperate need of the gospel. The church needs to learn to identify, network, encourage, and equip these marketspace workers and elevate their role in Great Commission work to the same level of validity as any commissioned missionary. Because they absolutely should be.

It is really not a new program.

Most missions organizations these days are talking about Business as Mission (BAM) as if it is a new venture — a new idea, and it very well may be for them. Business as Mission, however, is actually as old as the church's mission. Consider the explosion of the early church in the book of Acts. How did it come to be?

First off, we would be remiss not to begin this discussion about the expansion of the early church with the indwelling power and authority of the Holy Spirit. Jesus made it quite clear that apart from the strength and direction of the Holy Spirit, the church would simply never have gotten off the ground (Acts 1:4,8). The interesting thing, though, is who the Spirit used to grow the church and how.

The church was birthed in a miraculous display of God's sovereign power when the Spirit fell on Jews gathered in Jerusalem from around the world. Jesus' disciples began to proclaim his gospel in previously unknown languages so every person gathered there could understand it (Acts

2:5-11). The church grew by 3,000 people that day, and they soon returned to their homes. Thus, the spread of the gospel began. As the church grew, it was not necessarily well received. Faithful gospel proclamation and the spread of the church led to ever-increasing persecution by those outside its ranks. Christians, like Stephen, were martyred for their faith, causing many early Christians to flee Jerusalem and search out new places to live.

Families left and began new lives in new cities — working jobs, meeting neighbors, and living their faith all along the way. These were not the apostles; they were still in Jerusalem. They were simply people dispersed to the surrounding nations who lived as salt and light among those who were perishing. They had families to support, houses to build, and lives to share. And the church grew in their wake.

Acts 11 tells the story of the beginnings of the church in Antioch, and it is not what you might expect. There was no great missionary or evangelist or pastor who founded the church. It sprang up from the efforts of people who were dispersed from Jerusalem after Stephen's death. The church leaders in Jerusalem heard about what was happening there, and the thing that piqued their interest most was the fact that the gospel was crossing cultural barriers. Gentiles were coming to the faith. The church leaders sent Barnabas to check out what was happening, and he found Saul (who would later be called Paul) and brought him along. They did not, however, create the church; it existed before they arrived. People with regular jobs lived as salt and light and shared the good news across cultural bounds with great effectiveness, and the church in Antioch was born. So, whereas BAM may be fairly new in terms of missions organization initiatives, the practice is as ancient as the mission of the church itself.

Paul, along with his friends Aquila and Priscilla, also practiced marketspace missions. Acts 18 says of the trio: "After this Paul left Athens and went to Corinth. And he found a Jew named Aquila, a native of Pontus, recently come from Italy with his wife Priscilla, because Claudius had commanded all the Jews to leave Rome. And he went to see them, and because he was of the same trade he stayed with them and worked, for they were tentmakers by trade. And he reasoned in the synagogue every Sabbath, and tried to persuade Jews and Greeks. Each Sabbath found Paul at the synagogue, trying to convince the Jews and Greeks alike" (Acts 18:1-4).

Enter Paul the tentmaker, a man with a trade. According to this passage, Paul joined up with Aquila and Priscilla in their work. in other words, Paul got a job. He came into a new town, found some people with whom he shared a common trade, and began to work with them. So, during the week, he practiced a trade, and he spent the Sabbath in the synagogue reasoning with Jews. It can also be assumed that his work week was also a conduit for gospel interaction. Paul, it seems, practiced business as mission.

The pattern for Paul in his missionary efforts was to find an entry point from which he could launch his ministry. In this case, it was his business as a tentmaker and his status as a Pharisee, that gave him the ability to teach in the synagogue. At other times in his ministry, people and local churches brought him gifts that supported him, and he was able to exclusively give himself to preaching. Either one was acceptable to him. What that means for us today is that we need to elevate the one to the level of the other, because our default is to value "professional" missions over the salt and light witness of the otherwise "regular" person who simply works in the marketspace and lives out their faith wherever they are. For Paul, there was no hierarchy; neither should there be for us.

Currently, most of our churches ask business people to undertake "business-related" tasks within the church. They help out with accounting, sit on the administrative board, or help find a viable meeting space and negotiate the price. And while those are perfectly acceptable ways for them to serve the local body, it is far from all they can and should do.

They need to understand like Paul that their work is both a method of support for their primary identity as ambassadors of Christ and an avenue for engagement with people who are in desperate need of the gospel. They need to be encouraged and equipped to take full advantage of their talents and gifts in the marketplace for the glory of God, and that means far more than asking them to contribute to the current building project in their local church. **They have unique opportunities to share the gospel that others do not.** Again, like Paul, they need to be prepared to take full advantage of the opportunity to work as unto the Lord in the marketspace and share the glorious gospel of Christ with those people they come in contact with through their work.

But why did Paul need to do so? Ajith Fernando wrote in The NIV Application Commentary on the book of Acts that Paul most likely became a tentmaker for economic necessity and for credibility.[2] He had financial needs to be met. He also had a desire to maintain his credibility as a servant of Christ.[3] He worked in an age when philosophers and itinerant teachers were the norm, and they would often prey on people who were gullible and superstitious. They would charge people for services rendered, even when they produced no fruit. Paul wanted them to understand that the gospel message was different. Redemption by grace through faith was without cost, even if it meant that Paul had to find another way to support himself.

By Paul's day, the Cynic movement was widespread. The Cynic philosophers traveled from town to town, often preaching to crowds on street corners and in marketplaces. Their message was about a lifestyle free from want: totally non-materialistic. They depended on contributions for their basic needs. When they fell short of their financial goals, however, they often took advantage of gullible people. Paul wanted to make it clear that his aim was different because

[2] Ajith Fernando, The NIV Application Commentary on the book of Acts, 498 (Zondervan, 1998)

[3] Acts 20:34, 1 Cor. 4:12, 9:3-18, 1 Thess. 2:9, 2 Thess 3:8, 2 Cor. 11:7

of the gospel of Christ. Though it cost him everything, he wanted people to know that salvation cost them nothing. Paul worked hard to adapt to the context, as necessary, in order to make both his intentions and the gospel quite clear to his intended audience. He wanted to be sure to distance himself from the charlatan philosophers and teachers, and he did so by working hard to provide for himself.

Warren Wiersbe writes in his commentary that Paul separated himself from the "religious hucksters" by supporting himself as a tentmaker.[4] In this case, he met Aquila and Priscilla, who were Jewish and shared his trade.

Jewish rabbis did not accept money from their students, but earned their way by practicing a trade — and all Jewish boys were expected to learn a trade, no matter what profession they may enter. "He who does not teach his son to work, teaches him to steal," the rabbis said. Thus, it makes sense that Saul of Tarsus learned to make tents as a means of support for himself, even though his status in the Jewish world commanded support from the community (see Acts 18:3; 1 Cor. 9:6-15; 2 Cor. 11:6-10).

Furthermore, R.F. Hock writes, "According to some evidence, a number of Greek philosophers, beginning with Socrates, followed a pattern of witness in workshops and the marketspace; and Paul may well have utilized such an

[4] Wiersbe, Warren. The Wiersbe Bible Study Series. Acts. (Cook, 2010)

opportunity in exercising his own trade."[5] Not only was Paul's work a means of support, it was also an avenue for gospel ministry.

The second reason I cited above is that of credibility, which is one we can often overlook. As we've just seen, Paul was concerned with how the lost would view him, so much so that he plied his trade instead of asking for support — even though he had the right to do so.

There was a day in our modern culture in which pastors and religious workers were well-respected, simply because they filled those particular roles. Sadly, that day is long past. Our rapidly advancing post-Christian culture simply does not view religion and its leaders in the same way it once did. Add to that an almost never-ending onslaught of scandal and moral failure within the ranks of church leaders, and the hurdles for the full-time vocational Christian worker have grown increasingly higher by the day.

The church and its leaders have an image problem. We have violated the trust of the people, and our credibility is in the tank. Some people simply will not trust vocational ministers; so, the work rests in the hands of Christians in the marketspace. If this is true in our home culture, it must also be strongly considered in others.

In certain situations where there is not yet trust concerning

[5] Hock, R. F. The Workshop as a Social Setting for Paul's Missionary Preaching. CBQ 41 (1979)v 438-450

Christian missionaries, it is best for them not to take support from the people to whom they minister simply for the sake of developing trust (1 Corinthians 9).

Other cases will take workers into areas where the indigenous peoples simply cannot support a full-time vocational minister. These things are true of churches in poorer areas and in predominantly non-Christian cultures.[6]

When I read Ephesians 4:11-12, I know I have been guilty of thinking how I can better equip his people for the work of our church on Sunday mornings. I failed to see the global implications of these passages as we equip people in the marketspace. Listen to those words from Paul:

"So Christ himself gave the apostles, the prophets, the evangelists, the pastors and teachers, to equip his people for works of service, so that the body of Christ may be built up."

We shouldn't be solely focused on how we can build up the Sunday morning service. We shouldn't be limiting ourselves to the *inside* of the church building. Christ himself enabled us with the ability to equip believers for works of service, all for his glory. And what better work of service could there be than spreading the gospel?

Ruth Siemens authored an article entitled, "Tentmakers Needed for World Evangelization," in which she states that "tentmaking is becoming most valuable in today's world."

[6] Hock, 498.

In fact, she feels that the international job market (which is a key feature in today's business world) is an argument for tentmaking because, "it does not exist by accident but by God's design."[7] She describes it as God's repopulation program, transferring millions of hard-to-reach people into freer countries (Turks to Germany, Algerians to France, Kurds to Austria, etc.) and opening doors for Christians in hard to enter countries, so that many hear the gospel.

She further states, "the secular job is not an inconvenience, but the God-given context in which tentmakers live out the gospel in a winsome, wholesome, nonjudgmental way, demonstrating personal integrity, doing quality work and developing caring relationships."[8]

I know of some followers of Jesus who have intentionally moved to the inner city or to a remote area in their own country in order to be involved in church planting or evangelism. For instance, a church with which I am connected in the South asked members to consider taking jobs in an area outside the Bible belt where they supported a worker to plant a church. These "tentmakers" have greatly enhanced the work of the new church plant.

But we also must consider Aquila and Priscilla, who are described in Acts 18 as transnational marketspace workers. "After this Paul left Athens and went to Corinth. And

[7] Ruth Siemens, "Tentmakers Needed for World Evangelization," 1992.

[8] Siemens, 498.

he found a Jew named Aquila, a native of Pontus, recently come from Italy with his wife Priscilla, because Claudius had commanded all the Jews to leave Rome. And he went to see them, and because he was of the same trade he stayed with them and worked, for they were tentmakers by trade" (Acts 18:1-3).

Aquila was from Pontus, which is located in modern-day northern Turkey. Some scholars believe that Aquila may have been present at Pentecost. We do read in Acts 2:9 that Pontus was represented there among the nations listed in Jerusalem. We do not know for sure whether Aquila received the gospel there or later in Pontus from someone else.

The apostle Paul found Aquila and Priscilla in Corinth. They were recently expelled from Rome due to the uprising. Paul connected with them because they shared the same trade, tentmaking. In fact, it is where we get the term, "tentmaker." They received Paul into their home and he stayed with them and evidently worked with them. They connected with each other through the marketspace. They had a natural affinity through their work.

Think about how this plays out today: when you meet people, one of the first things you start talking about is where you are from and what is your profession. When I tell people I am a pastor, it often takes the conversation in a definite direction. If the person I am meeting is a pastor, then we can start talking about a large range of subjects. But if I meet an engineer or a pharmaceutical representative, then our conversation has to connect at a level other than work.

Neither Luke nor Paul ever mentioned in their writings that Aquila and Priscilla were in full-time ministry. I think this is significant. This leads me to think that they were involved in marketspace ministry. Consider another important aspect: we read about them in four different cities (Pontus, Rome, Corinth, and Ephesus). They evidently had the skills and ability to move from place to place to practice their trade.

Later in Acts 18:18, we see that Aquila and Priscilla went with Paul and eventually ended up in Ephesus. As marketspace workers, their intentionality was crucial. No matter where they lived, they were engaged in the work of the gospel.

- They were coworkers with Paul in Christ Jesus (Romans 16:3)
- They risked their lives for Paul (Romans 16:4)
- The church was extremely grateful for them (Romans 16:3)
- They assisted Paul in Ephesus (Acts 18:18-28)
- They hosted a church in their own home (1 Cor. 16:19, Romans 16:3-5)
- They instructed Apollos privately to help him to learn more about Jesus (Acts 18:26)

"Here is a perfect example before us — by Christians like Aquila and Priscilla traveling the routes of trade and commerce and carrying their faith wherever they went," writes John B. Polhill.[9] The intentionality shown by Aquila and Priscilla went beyond their workplace. It also extended into their community, as they showed hospitality, especially in their home. In Scripture, we see the following examples of their hospitality:

- A church met in their home (1 Corinthians 16:19, Romans 16:5).
- They must have demonstrated hospitality. We see where Paul stayed with them as they shared the same trade (Acts 18:3).
- They invited Apollos to their house so they could explain more about Jesus to him (Acts 18:26).

Marketspace professionals do many things on the mission field. They share their faith with not-yet believers. They are disciplemakers wherever they live, work or play. They lead or help with the planting of new churches, minister to those in need, involve their sending churches in partnering overseas, and start Bible studies. They make intentional choices in their daily lives and come alongside one another to pray, encourage, mentor, and learn as they serve in the marketspace, carrying on the legacy left by Aquila and Priscilla.[10]

While most write about Paul and his tentmaking examples, I want to make people who live more like Aquila and

[9] Polhill, John B. The American Commentary. Acts.
[10] Siemens, Tentmakers, D-247.

Priscilla the focus of this book. They are my heroes. They are people who are literally salt and light as Jesus talked about. They did so wherever they lived. Whatever context they found themselves in. Unfortunately, often we celebrate only the ones who are ordained and appointed. We miss the unbelievable opportunities in a global marketspace to make disciples — ones who find it normal to take the transfer to another country and be salt and light.

Way too often, we hear of people who would love to have their church support them while working overseas, but they learn their church only does that for those they classify as full-time missionaries. This book celebrates those who are or who had the opportunity to do this. It is also for you — the man or woman who is called to live on mission in another country. God may be opening doors for you right now to work overseas with a real job. You are needed!

WE NEED TO GET OUT OF THE WAY

I remember speaking one day at an extremely traditional church. I was asked to talk about our work and so I talked about how normal people can use their skills and their jobs to plant the gospel, no matter where they are. I prepared well for the message. I had all of my points. I really felt like I needed to lay a strong foundation for this idea.

After the message, I was down front and talking to several people about it. It dawned on me after several comments that the lay people get this. It makes sense to them. No matter what style the church is, I found that many lay people can easily buy in. They just need permission. Guess where they feel they are not getting permission? Often, from people like me — the paid professionals. Somehow, we have decided that pastors and professional missionaries are the answer. We propel the notion that the gospel will be spread by these missionaries, when in fact, the Great Commission was given to the church and to all followers of Jesus.

This is not anything radical. It is simply the norm.

Take the gospel every place you go.

However, I usually get a lot of comments and questions from pastors who tell me they have never considered this before now and it opens new realms of possibilities for them as a church. Think about it. On a week-in and week-out basis they are discipling their people to love Jesus and follow him. To live like Jesus lives. To take the gospel to their neighbors and workplace. Why do we stop there? Why do we tell people they need to quit their jobs and get theological training and raise support to be a full-time missionary?

Where did we come up with that?

Although it may sound like it, I really do not have a lot against the modern missionary movement. I am all in when it comes to taking the gospel to the nations. I just don't believe that the only pathway is a full-time vocational missionary pathway.

Another time, I was speaking with a young couple who was preparing to go with a missionary-sending agency to a country in Europe. The husband worked for a multinational company. I asked him to talk about his calling and to define his vision. As I did, he realized he didn't know what he would tell people in Europe that he did. I suggested he not resign his job and give up his income and reason to be somewhere, but simply ask for a transfer — go global with your company. He believed the only way he could be a missionary was to be sent by an organization to work full time as a church planter.

I ran into that guy about a year later, and he lamented that he was having such a hard time explaining to his neighbors why he was living in their country. He had no natural ways of connecting with the very people he was trying to take the gospel to. He longed for the day where he could go to his regular job and be a normal person who takes the gospel wherever he goes.

When most people arrive on the field, they suddenly realize they don't know how to describe what they do to their new neighbors and friends. Sometimes, these people are not really fond of them being in their country, anyway. In this case, the man learned this from his pastor.

The couple did not take my advice, and that is fine, but I wonder what would happen if more followers of Christ would be open to living anywhere in the world and seek out regular jobs where they can be salt and light.

What needs to be changed? Our way of processing. We need to give people permission. We need to view what they are doing as a valid expression of missionary involvement. The church needs to do this. Missionaries need to embrace this. We need to help them live effectively in cross-cultural situations. We need to train them in church planting. We need to help them with theological training, but they do not need to quit their day job.

The delivery of theological education is changing for the good. These men and women are smart. They can do it. We just need to get out of the way and let them. What if in our church we started thinking of mobilizing marketspace people, students and retirees? What if we started pooling these types of workers and started to develop and train them to go to the nations? What if we created systems in our churches where we would pray for them, care for them, hold them accountable, and ensure that they are connected to strategic opportunities abroad? Honestly, they could teach us a few things about connecting with people wherever they live, work and play. After all, they are doing it each day.

PART TWO: A LEGITIMATE REASON TO BE THERE AND THE MEANS TO STAY

WHICH PATHWAY IS BEST FOR ME?

It is not only important that a person find a legitimate reason to serve overseas, but he or she also has to find a way to stay there — a sustainable way for the amount of time he or she will be living abroad.

But this section is not just for the potential worker. The church also needs to be involved, because its members are the ones who will shepherd and equip the worker in the best way possible. Who could assess the potential of a person better than the church?

The missions organization and the missionary also need to be involved. It is equally important for the church to send well and the missionary team to receive well, bringing these workers into community and strategic involvement as team members.

At this point, if you are dreaming of working overseas, you're probably asking, "What is the best pathway for me?" This is a question I often receive from people in the church interested in going overseas to live intentionally. There are multiple pathways to being salt and light in a cross-cultural context. Let's explore a few of these.

INTENTIONAL TRAVELERS

I do a lot of traveling. I mean, more than most, but not quite as much as George Clooney in the Hollywood film *Up in the Air.* I am constantly in conversations with people who are doing business all over the world. They fly about from country to country. They work for multinational companies. They often have to travel to the same cities several times a year with their jobs. They want to be intentional as they travel and do business abroad. They do not simply want to go on a trip to do their business and see a few sights.

One business person stays at the same bed and breakfast each time in Paris. He plans ahead to be sure the owners of the hotel can spend one evening with him. He frequents the same restaurants. Goes to the same newsstand each morning to get his paper. Visits the same coffee shops. He makes sure to spend time with people from his national company. He goes out to eat with his co-workers. He gets to know them as well as possible. He is trying to learn the language in order to communicate better in that country.

WE NEED TO VIEW WHAT THEY ARE DOING AS A VALID EXPRESSION OF MISSIONARY INVOLVEMENT.

He is meeting other Christians and Christian workers to develop his network there. He tries to make the most of his opportunities, and if the Lord opens the doors for deeper conversations, then he is ready. Though this guy probably won't live overseas, he knows that a real part of his life is to travel abroad. He is committed to making it intentional.

What does this take? Trying to learn the language at some level. Planning ahead for your trip. Doing some research of the area where you are staying and learning about the people who live there. Once you are there, make prayer walking a normal part of your day. Keep track of your contacts there and be sure to alert them when you are traveling nearby so you can have a meal or drink with them.

The key to this type of traveler is intentionality. They do not go on trips haphazardly. They seek the Lord's guidance. They seek out opportunities. They pray for open doors. From time to time, we run into business people who contact us and say, "I am going to be in such and such city for a week doing business. I would love to connect with a ministry while I'm there to see if I can be of an encouragement or help strategically." This person truly can make a difference.

Missionaries: How can you proactively be ready for such workers who come into your city? Here are some ideas:

1. Prepare a prayer guide via podcast or print and send it to the business traveler who is coming your way.
2. Think about possible ways you could partner with a

business person who is coming to your city. Do they possess certain skills you could utilize in your work among the people there?

3. Are there friends you could introduce them to who would be interested in hearing their story?
4. Are there certain projects you can plug them into?
5. Are there national believers or churches you may know that you can introduce them to?

The effectiveness of this pathway often depends on if they can partner with an on-the-ground team of people who is taking the gospel to that city. With some prior communication, strategic insight, good connections, and follow-up, this type of marketspace ministry can make significant gains for both the worker and the missionary.

Churches: What if you begin to ask where your people travel for work? I know a church that created an interactive map so that their marketspace people could pin the places they go for business. They were then able to help them make strategic introductions where desired. You could equip them for starting gospel conversations, sharing the gospel, and even missionary strategies.

What if your church starts a group that meets quarterly with global travellers so they can share where they are going on a regular basis, pray together, think through strategic opportunities, and learn ways they can share their faith?

What if your church worked to find strategic field partners

for your members working overseas on business trips so they can have some strategic connections, support as needed, not to mention for them to provide care and community in some instances with the field partners?

THE TRANSFER / THE EXPAT COMMUNITY

A great way to get a job overseas is to receive a job transfer. The only problem with this is that many people are not currently working for companies that send employees abroad. Landing that overseas job with your company can be a tough proposition. It sounds a lot easier than it is. If you are serious about wanting to work in the marketspace overseas, look for jobs at companies with offices or factories abroad.

Jay and his family are from the Midwest. He was climbing the corporate ladder in his company, doing well, but never really thought about going overseas. One day, he got a notice from his boss that said he and his family would be moving to Germany. The company told him he would be moving in about a month, so he had to get everything ready pretty quickly for at least a 4 to 5 year job assignment. They were enthusiastic about it. He had been on mission trips before, and had always wondered if God had been calling him into full-time missions. But he found his young family being transferred to Germany instead, through his large German company. He asked if there was some sort of missionary team or church-planting team that he could be involved with. We made some contacts and inquiries and, sure enough, there was a German church plant in the very town in which he was moving. We were able to connect him and his family. They joined this church plant and have been involved there for the past four or five years. They have lived out their lives missionally as a family in their German town. They learned the language. They learned the culture. They connected with people in their city. They have served the church well.

The leader of a large corporation in East Asia gave me some great advice once. He recommended people find a job in a global company, while still living in the States. "When you begin employment, let them know you are interested in working overseas. Then pray for opportunities," he urged. Being an asset to your company will make them more likely to offer you global job opportunities.

One person who worked for an American company in Europe said that most companies won't even look at sending you until you've worked for their company for five to eight years. When they start offering you jobs, be ready to say yes to the first posting. They will not keep offering you job transfers if you always say no. See where God takes you.

One possible downside to this approach is when you sense a calling to go to a certain nation, you do not always have the ability to take a job where you desire. You have to go where your company sends you. But don't be discouraged. You never know what doors will open when you leave all that is familiar to venture out into the world. Trust in the Holy Spirit's guidance and the sovereignty of the missionary God.

Missionaries: One way you could be proactive in such a scenario is to map out the global companies in your city. You could actually do a little homework and find out where their headquarters are located, then seek out partner churches that may have members who work in those companies.

Churches: Consider creating a "sending pipeline," or a guide to encourage members to explore different avenues for spreading the gospel. As you create your pipeline, identify multiple pathways to develop: vocational missionaries, students, marketspace workers, business startups, English as a Second Language teachers, other careers in the education sector, etc. As you identify these pools of people in your church, you can start casting vision for them to find ways to take their jobs to the nations. The Upstream Collective actually has a resource that can help you do this, titled "Developing a Sending Pipeline."

MANAGEMENT OR MID-LEVEL MANAGEMENT IN ANOTHER COUNTRY

When an international company asks you to come and work for them, they are not usually thinking about a 40-hour work week. In most cases, the hours will be quite demanding and the expectations high. They likely need an English speaker to fill the place in their company to give them an edge. However, if you can land a job in an international city, there are a variety of ways you can connect. You may decide that being a part of a national or international church is the best route for you. In larger cities, there are often churches you can participate in and this will give you the opportunity for good community. If this is your desire, find a church with an active outreach ministry and get involved in local outreach. I have seen in some international churches the same thing that happens here in the States: most of the volunteer opportunities have to do with the Sunday service.

In other cases, you may want to join an existing missionary team. We will talk more about that as we move into the book. Missionary teams will often be focused on the task of what is called "zero to one" evangelism. They are trying to take the gospel to places and people in that city where it has not been heard. They will often engage in a variety of ways and can be a place where your support and efforts could be greatly used. You will most likely need to begin learning language in this type of effort, but you really should be doing that anyway.

Churches: What if you help the person who is getting a job in a new country by connecting them with a missionary team or local church? This is where churches developing deep partnerships with sending agencies can really come into play. With a strong relationship, the church can reach out to the sending agency to find out if they have a team there. As churches identify themselves more and more with networks of churches, these networks have become global, and you can find churches within your network all over the world.

JOB SEARCHERS

Often this can be the hardest part of the equation. How do I find a job? Where should I look? We have learned a few things over the last four years regarding landing that job. If you're currently job searching, this may be just what you need. If you are in the position to help people explore this pathway to missions and they are looking for a job, please pass this along. It can be very helpful in finding work overseas. How can we as pastors, missionaries, or professors help our students prepare for this type of work? These are some things you should consider:

1. Choose your major. If you are wanting to work abroad, your university years are a great time to start preparing. Do some research on the job market overseas. Look into various sectors that interest you and talk to expats on the ground. From there, you can make a wise and informed choice for your major. For example, some useful areas of study include:

- ESL Teacher
- Translator/Interpreter
- Engineering
- Pharmaceutical Research
- International Business
- Information Technology (IT)
- Coding
- Graphic Design

Adding a strategic minor, such as foreign language or

business, can also open doors and improve your chances. Internships and semesters abroad should be considered as well.

2. Learn another language. Ask anyone in human resources, and they'll tell you that North Americans looking to work abroad have a great advantage: they are native English speakers. But they'll also tell you that you should speak at least one other language well. Depending on the region that interests you, this could be a major business language such as Spanish, Arabic, Mandarin, or French.

3. Experience life abroad. Study abroad programs abound, and they vary widely in destination, focus, duration, and cost. Make an appointment with your college/university study abroad advisor, or look into an independent program or language school. If the option exists, consider staying with a host family to maximize the international experience and get first-hand exposure to the language, culture, and values of the country. This kind of experience can really boost your résumé, even if you are applying for a job in another region of the world than your study abroad experience.

4. Do an internship overseas. It's true that you may not find a paying internship opportunity, but if at all possible, find a way to dip your toes in the international job market. It will probably take some networking, and maybe even some waiting tables to pay the bills, but an internship abroad will pay off by showing future employers that you are motivated and experienced.

Although it may seem easier (and it probably is) to get an internship in your current city, consider looking for one overseas. Working as an intern in another country will open you up to countless experiences, one of them being that you may be offered a job. At the very least, you will be well-networked to know how to find a job in that country, and who is hiring. Because you will have already worked in that environment, people will be much more likely to consider you, even though you are a foreigner. They will see that you are not just some outsider, but someone who has spent time and energy in their country or place of business.

5. Ask, and be flexible. If you work for a multinational company, or are interviewing with one, ask their human resources department about possible job openings overseas. By proactively asking and showing your interest, you'll stand out! Here's a tip from a VP in a large company: when the HR representative asks where you are willing to go, be willing to go anywhere! The kind of people they want to hire for overseas jobs are flexible and adaptable.

6. Accept short work assignments. Quite often in international companies, you may first be asked to go overseas on a one-year assignment, or possibly even a shorter duration. Take it! Prove yourself to be a capable, effective overseas worker. Only then will you get the assignments that allow you to stay overseas, maybe even in the same location, for years at a time.

7. Join a guild or professional organization. As you focus on a field of study or career path, find out if there are any professional organizations or guilds you can join, such as an artist guild or acting guild. Sometimes these memberships can open doors for interviews and opportunities for visas to work abroad, which is no small feat in most countries.

8. Look in person. It is a lot easier to find an overseas job if you are, in fact, overseas. The internet is a great tool, but spending some time on the ground and in person is often more effective than emails or phone calls. In most countries, as a North American, you can stay for up to three months on a tourist visa.

9. Ask for connections. Make the most of international networking opportunities. Who do you know in that country? Who do you know working in that field? Can these people connect you with companies that are hiring? It all starts with asking.

10. Attend job fairs. Across North America, there are several annual job fairs focused on working abroad. Look online for the one nearest you and make a point to attend, to ask questions and to meet people.

11. Be open. Sometimes the most obvious option for you may not be what God will use to move you overseas. It's very easy for a person to get tunnel vision about how they will make something happen, especially something like a move abroad. Being open about job opportunities also means being open about location.

One couple attended an international job fair for teachers and went into the weekend with a big desire to go to one country. They had already met with the administrators of the school in that country and felt like it would be a good fit for them. However, over the course of the weekend, they looked into additional teaching positions at schools located in other countries where their church had more of a strategic focus. They ended up accepting a job offer at a completely different school in order to better facilitate the mission of their sending church.

ENTREPRENEURS

Another pathway into a different country is the entrepreneur. This pathway gets a lot of press. It is the one most people think of when they think of moving overseas. An entrepreneur finds a way to get in by starting a business or bringing business with them. They have an idea and they are just wired to start a company. Do you like to start something from nothing? Do you have a dream for something that could work? Can you write out a business plan and execute it? If so, this may be the pathway for you.

Many people think they are an entrepreneur, but in actuality they are not. Not to be critical, but ideas come pretty easy. Executing them and turning them into a profit-making business is something a bit more challenging. Look back in your own life. Can you find examples in your life where you have started something from nothing? Have you ever started a company?

If you answered no to these two questions, it does not mean you cannot do it. It may mean you just need some coaching to turn your ideas into a viable business. Your church may be a great place to get the coaching you need. Connect with business owners in your church and ask them to speak into your life. Consider asking for business coaching.

If you have an interest in starting a company, get to know the area where you want to start the company. Learn about their business regulations and laws. Most countries have a guide on their consulate website. It will let you know if you can start a company and how to go about doing it. Another resource is to look at the American Chamber of Commerce for that country or city. You can find out valuable information from them.

Research your idea to see if it can fly where you are wanting to start. I remember talking to a person once who had an idea to start a tourist-related company in a large European city. As they were pitching the idea, I was multitasking and researching it online. I was on Skype and they couldn't see that I had the mute button on (don't tell me you do not do that!). As I was researching this idea, I found that there were already at least five companies of the same idea operating in that city. They did not have a niche. They were entering into an already crowded market. Usually new business start ups or expansions are filling niches that are not being met currently in that country. They also can provide job opportunities for locals which can support the local economy.

If you have the initial business capital to start the business, it can be sustainable from an income perspective, at least for the short term. Most countries would require you to have a certain amount of cash or capital in order to begin.

This pathway could be inflexible in that a lot of your time could be spoken for. You would need to work hard at starting a business and that usually entails long days. Depending on the type of business, it could put you squarely among the people you are wanting to engage — or your business may be great in a sustainable way, but put you far away from the people you are wanting to engage. For example, if you were starting a coffee shop in Europe, hoping to engage immigrants and refugees there, then your coffee shop probably wouldn't be in their neighborhood. Your customers would most likely be nationals and international expats who could afford a $4 latte.

This does not mean it is a bad idea, but if it is not getting you access to the people you want to reach, then you must make intentional choices to live in or near the neighborhoods you are wanting to engage and free your time to access those people in meaningful ways. The ideal here is to be able to start a company, directly engaging people with whom you are deciding to share the gospel.

But I do know people who have explored various ways to start a company overseas and were successful. They usually do a lot of homework on the front end, both here and abroad. They normally make several trips to the city they are considering — to explore the land, meet people, and look into similar businesses, if any. They come back and put together a business plan and start finding investors to start their new company. We tend to see a high effectiveness rate for a person to start a company and register it in the States before going global with it.

For people looking to start a business that could take them overseas, a great tool is *The $100 Startup* by Chris Guillebeau. This book tells story after story of how ordinary people took a passion and turned it into a profitable business. Guillebeau surveyed and interviewed hundreds of entrepreneurs for the making of the book and he limited it to those that made a least $50k each year, and started their business with no more than $1,000. A great majority of his examples actually started their businesses on less than $100. This book can be a good resource because it lays out the basic steps a person can take as they explore the idea of starting their own business. With helpful chapters like, "The One-Page Business Plan" or "How to Franchise Yourself," anyone who has an entrepreneurial bent will enjoy this book and find it helpful as they attempt to start a business that could take them overseas.

I am extremely grateful for one such businessman who is quite an entrepreneur. Though he would shy away from any credit, I feel like his story is worth telling. We'll call him Dan.

Dan owns a growing mid-sized company that he started from scratch. He has been very successful throughout the last 15 years. God has blessed him in some unique ways.

Recently, Dan had some extra office space and decided to donate this space to Christian ministries. He let a new church plant use the space until they found their own. Currently, the space is used as a missions network office.

Not only has Dan donated to other churches, he has also helped his own church develop a business as mission strategy. Much of its effort has been helping Christian entrepreneurs living overseas do a better job with their businesses. Often we full-time missionaries are not the best business people (I know that may come as a surprise to some of my readers)! This guy takes at least two trips a year to help out these types of workers. Not too long ago, he put together a group of business people to go overseas for a week of business coaching.

In his city of business, he is also involved in a network of leaders who are serious about business as mission. They meet monthly to plan and implement business strategies overseas that will help send out workers, sustain workers and companies, and more.

Dan initiated a quarterly event in his city that celebrates these stories of business as mission and helps these men and women discover their next steps, whether they are in that city or another part of the world.

But perhaps Dan's most impressive quality is his magnetism. His employees really enjoy working for him. He has created a great environment for the workplace in a very profitable business.

He helps fund his employees' mission trips. They must use their own vacation time, which I totally think is a great idea. It hinders employees from abusing the time as a vacation-oriented trip. It demonstrates the employee's commitment to the mission as well. They adopt a ministry in the city to invest in, supplying resources and volunteering. All of this is voluntary on the part of the employee, but it gives them some projects and partnerships to be involved in.

While I am writing Dan's biography, I can't forget to include how he lives this out day to day. Dan and I share a common interest. We are foodies. We love to go to the outermost places of the city, the distant places that most do not traverse. Now I love going to these places because it makes me feel at home. It is odd that after living abroad for so many years, home does not feel like home anymore, but another culture feels like home.

As we go into these places and eat, Dan usually just says a simple prayer of blessing for the place and the people who work there. It is quite like Luke 10:5-6a: "Whatever house you enter, first say, 'Peace be to this house!' And if a son of peace is there, your peace will rest upon him."

It is amazing how God is blessing this guy with relationships and spiritual conversations. You truly see the fruit of a man who is following God with all of his heart and his vocation. Dan may never live overseas. I am convinced he would do quite well, but he may actually be more effective here. He has found ways to do business as mission in his own community.

What if you started a company that was intentional about starting other companies in difficult places? What if you set up a recruitment company that focused on getting jobs for Christ followers all over the world? What if you started a company that researched and recommended best places in the world for business start ups? What if?

What type of company would you start? The sky's the limit!

THE BUSINESS EXPANSION

Many companies are looking to expand their markets and to go to other parts of the world. What if the business owners and decision makers did this with intentionality? What if they sought out from the Lord where they should start such endeavors? What could this look like?

Countries often offer visas to business workers who wish to explore the potential of starting a new company branch. What if we were intentional and strategic about this type of expansion?

I learned of a kingdom-minded business owner who heard of a few people sensing a calling to go overseas. He resonated with their idea of being business people in this particular city ... so much so that he decided he needed to open a viable branch for his company. He found a couple of these men to be good employees in their new overseas venture. Often, we need to just plant the seed of the idea for business people to take it and expand their companies into global markets.

If you are a business owner, can I challenge you regarding the tension of making a lot of money versus making a decent profit? What is your goal? What kind of profit do you need to make in order for it to be worth your investment of time and finances? This may not sound very capitalistic, but we need to adjust our money-making expectations. Please do not hear me wrong. We need to start companies or expand companies to be profitable — but how profitable? Do we need to only invest in companies that would make a lot of money, or are we willing to take on some projects or even expansions at a smaller profit margin?

RETIREES

This pathway is often a challenge. It sounds like a good idea conceptually, but the reality is that by the time a person hits retirement age, they may not feel ready to move. However, many countries have visa regulations that would allow them to live in their country.

A key question to ask if you feel called to a certain country is, "Will it make sense to the locals to retire there?" Sure, it is obvious you would want to retire in France, Australia, or Indonesia. But does it make sense to the locals if you are choosing to retire in Chad or China? It may, but most likely you may need another reason to live there. What if you retired there, but were also able to volunteer for a non-profit organization that helps the people of that country? Now it makes sense.

If you are choosing this pathway, you need to take U.S. Social Security rules and tax rules into account. I have seen some people go this route for a shorter season, like one to three years.

Another challenge: often, when one is entering retirement age, life circumstances become complicated and emotionally challenging. You may have aging parents who need more care and attention. And if you have children or grandchildren, it may be hard to be absent from them.

Overall, this pathway is underutilized and deserves more attention from the church. In many cases, churches have been so focused on sending long-term missionaries that we have underdeveloped plans for what is called the "mid-term worker." This is where a person or family only plans to stay in the country up to two years. There may be challenges, but there are even greater benefits.

The ability to serve alongside a younger team could open up strategic access that the existing team could not engage. In many cultures, the older person is given more respect. Out of cultural respect, people may give you a hearing. I heard of a retired pastor who served in Africa for several years after retirement. He worked in a rural area and was able to talk to many of the people who lived there, simply because they respected older men. You might be the key they need to open new doors.

ARTISANS

It is amazing to me that many countries will allow people with certain skills to live and work there. It may be hard to earn enough to live on and may require you to adjust your lifestyle standards, but it can work. Whether you are a barista, a farmer, a musician, or a craftsman, you can move your business to a new country.

I have seen people who are members of certain guilds or have specific certifications able to live in a country to practice their art. It does take a legitimate amount of business skill in being able to market and sell your work, but for some, this is the exact pathway they need to take.

This type of work gives great flexibility of time. You are often out among the people. You have the chance to be a learner. Instead of simply trying to create and sell your own style, what if you learn the style of the people you are living among? You could create art that makes sense to the people. Or look at it as another opportunity: what if you are able to not just sell your art, but also find ways to help locals sell their art?

TEACHERS

Many countries desire native English speakers to come to their country and teach English. It is currently still the global business language. In many countries, schools for children and adults are actively seeking people to come and teach. It can often require long hours to have a sustainable income, but in some cases, schools will hire you and pay you a good wage. One advantage of this pathway is that it puts you in contact with the people. It makes sense for you to be there and say you are an English teacher or that you teach at a school. In many cases, it gives you great flexibility in your hours, so you can devote more time to a team strategy.

If you are interested in this pathway, then it is best to have a college degree or a certification to teach English as a Second Language. I highly recommend that if you go the certification route, get a certification that is recognized internationally. You can do a quick search on the internet to find such options.

FREELANCE WORKERS

Freelance work is one of the most flexible pathways in this group. With the right skill set and good clients or contracts, you can work overseas yet have the flexibility to work when you want. You can schedule your work hours to work when others are working, but have the ability to be off during their off times to engage with the people. In many developed countries, you can also rent out office space and have the ability to share a workspace.

You need to consider the accessibility factor. If you are working alone or out of your house, then you will not be with the people. While this may be great in giving you the time needed to work with your team, you may not get to spend time with locals in their workplace. Having a work space outside of your home naturally enables you to connect more with the people. I know of several people who are going this route with their freelance work and it seems to work well for them in relation to developing work relationships, connecting with people, and providing much-needed community in their own lives. Sharing a workspace could be a great solution.

STUDENTS

Another pathway to consider is that of being a student and living intentionally while studying there. This is a great idea for churches who have certain cities or places where they are trying to engage. The church can mobilize their students to study for a semester in the place where they are strategically involved, or where they have long-term workers from their church serving. Some students studied abroad with a partnership from their university to the city they were wanting to live. They lived there for three to six months and connected with a missionary team.

I have also seen students decide to complete their entire degree overseas or go back to obtain their master's and/or doctoral degrees. They typically learn the language well in this type of situation. As a student, they have credibility to be there. They usually have flexibility in their study schedule and often have weekends free. They are able to live there with scholarships, or in some cases, their parents' resources.

However, there are challenges with this pathway. They may have to be very intentional where they live in order to engage with the people their team is working with. Unless of course, their missionary team is working with university students. In that case, it is a total win-win.

Another consideration is that of finances. They may need some income to be sustainable. They may need to acquire part-time jobs for living expenses or perhaps even raise a portion of their funds to live there missionally.

Liz had a heart for the nations when she was younger and in college and she ended up finishing up her under-graduate studies at a prestigious university in England. She was able to start working on her Ph.D. by getting accepted into a school in Freiburg, Germany. We caught up with Liz because she was a member of a church that we were help-ing to plant. She was an integral part of the core group in this early church plant. She was very much involved in her work and her research project, but also found ways to live as salt and light among the people she worked around, and she also served this church plant in some great capacities.

SPOUSES OF VISA HOLDERS

An often overlooked person is the spouse of the visa holder. They are not usually granted a work visa, so they could have more flexibility with their time. If they are younger and have children, then they will most likely be the one helping with the kids during the day.

Generally, we tend to disregard the spouse because we traditionally think of marketspace workers as people who work or Business as Mission being the pathway to engagement. But what about finding ways to equip, empower, and release the spouse? They often have skills that could be utilized on the team. They may have more time to invest in team projects. They often will have access to people that you are not able to engage.

If you are a spouse of a worker, talk about what this could look like for you as a couple. Talk with the missionary team about opportunities for you to minister as well. Discover ways you can reach people using the gifts and skills God has given you.

Note to the Missionary: While this section focused on the worker finding an effective pathway that suits them and potential ways to make it on the ground, I also want to mention a few places you should look to find such workers.

First, start with prayer. Pray for readiness on your part and for your team for this type of worker. Pray that God will send you people who desire to work with you and the people group you are engaging.

You also need to know where to look. We often miss low-hanging fruit. I am not a farmer, but I do remember hiking some trails in Germany that bordered strawberry fields, blueberry patches, and apple orchards. I was told by a local that, as a traveler, I was permitted to take a piece of the fruit to eat along the way. I never tried this because my father told me never to take something that did not belong to me. But, in theory, I liked this idea. We actually see this in the Old Testament, where the sojourner could eat from the edges of the field. This is an example of low-hanging fruit.

There are often people whom God has given to this type of work right in your own city. Believers may live there, longing to enlist in ministry in this manner. As you develop relationships with local or international churches, offer to help these churches engage their community by mobilizing and equipping marketspace people who are already there.

Another place to search would be sending churches in the States. Ask your sending churches or partners if they have members of their congregation who would desire to take their life and work overseas.

One other place to look is within your own missions organization. They are often looking for ways to mobilize marketspace workers and it would be helpful for them to know you are desirous of having such workers on your team.

They may have a list of people interested in moving overseas.

Marketspace Worker: Before we move on to the next section, I want to show you a chart that can help you think through the various pathways and the strategic implications that you should consider. Use this chart to pray through your options and to plan which pathway to utilize.

	Student Study abroad, Masters Level, language	Retiree	Business Owner or Start Up	Mid-Management or Management Job Transfer	Artisan Artist, Craft, Barista	Teacher ESL, National School	Spouse of Visa Holder	Freelancer Coding, IT Web Design, Graphic Artist, Editor
Accessibility								
Will I have access to the people I feel drawn to engage?								
Am I able to get a visa to live there legally?								
Flexibility								
Are your hours flexible for work or study?								
How many hours are you expected to work each week?								
Sustainability								
Does it provide enough income to live on with-out support raised?								
Credibility								
Does your job make sense to the people who live there?								
What type of weight will the people put on the type of job you have?								
Geographical								
Will you be able to live close to the people you are engaging?								

PART THREE: TRAINING THE SENDING CHURCH, MARKETSPACE WORKER, AND MISSIONARY TEAM

I like to think of myself as a person who prepares for what lies ahead. For example, I know that if I have a meeting at 10 a.m. to discuss planning for one of our ministry's training events, I will write out my notes and questions for whoever I am meeting with. I will usually confirm the appointment. I will be sure to be prepared. But for whatever reason, I will often forget to actually get directions on how to arrive. Over time, I have learned that if I cut and paste the address into my calendar, all I have to do is push a button and the directions and best route magically appear. I am also aware that the success of my meeting also lies in the hands of the person with whom I am meeting. Are they prepared for the meeting? Have they brought their questions? Have they brought examples or illustrations of their plan? The bottom line is that it takes preparation to go somewhere, and it takes the other person being prepared as well.

In this section, we will be discussing how the sending church needs to prepare their sent ones. We will look at how the missionary or missionary team must prepare to receive well. Later, in the last section of the book, we will look at how the marketspace worker can be strategic, and the skills it would be helpful to learn as they go. We will also look at how the marketspace worker needs to prepare not just to survive in their new role overseas, but to actually thrive.

I think preparation for these types of pathways starts with the on-the-ground missionary. The reason I say this is because often integrating a marketspace worker into a field team is hard. It sounds good for the home office of the mission organization to say we need marketspace workers to come from good sending churches. But it also takes the field worker being ready. They need to be prepared to receive this different type of worker well.

PREPARE FOR THEIR ARRIVAL

How can you, as a vocational missionary, prepare for the arrival of someone who is moving to your city?

After reflecting on our last move, my wife Susan and I wrote a book called *First 30 Daze: Practical Encouragement for Living Abroad Intentionally.* It is a play on the word "days," because you may remember that when you move to a new culture you are literally in a daze. I know we have been each time we have moved. I know this may sound like a shameless plug, but I believe this book can help people thrive. For more than 15 years, we incorporated new team members into our team. In some cases, they were full-time missionaries, but in other cases, they were marketspace workers and students or retirees. In every case they needed community, accountability, mentoring, strategic focus, and direction. Think of *First 30 Daze* as a field journal, guidebook, and devotional, all in one. It would be helpful for you, the sending church, and of course, the marketspace worker to read this book.

Secondly, I would recommend developing a list that can help you determine some activities and tasks someone will need to consider as they move overseas. This will help you figure out what needs to be done in preparation and what questions you have that you would like to see addressed before their arrival. If you are thinking proactively about receiving a new teammate, then you will most likely be better prepared in receiving them well and integrating them into your team. The list should focus heavily on addressing logistical questions. This will be heavy on the minds of the people moving overseas. Remember back when you first moved overseas. Sure, you were interested in strategy, but you also needed a plan for arrival, where you will live, etc.

This will give them some items to consider, like:

- Where to live, based on strategy more than convenience
- What are the different schooling options for their children
- What they can buy there versus what they should bring with them
- Where the ministry team lives and focuses its effort
- What are some of the international moving options

If they are coming with an international company, then they may get many of these questions answered by their international moving consultants or their human resource department.

However, if they are coming as a student, retiree, self-funded, or bringing their job with them, then it is more likely they will need more help. Many of these questions are not super hard to answer, but they will take some time and they are tremendously important for the people coming. You have the opportunity and responsibility to help them. If you are planning on having several of this type of worker come to your city, you could begin an FAQ sheet to avoid duplicating your work each time.

Dialogue about where they live, if you can. This can be a sensitive subject. To be honest, no one wants to be told where to live — but it is highly important. If they are working with nationals and you have a church planting or missions effort taking place in a certain part of the city and your existing team lives in that area, then you may want to have them closer by. It would be easier for team projects and easier to have community with one another, which is one of our key components of the marketspace worker.

In many cases, we find that large global companies outsource the moving to local real estate partners. This is helpful for the worker moving over, but often they will give misguided advice. The companies usually recommend living near other expats or international schools. If you can build the rapport with them to be able to speak into that, then you may be able to encourage them to look nearer your location.

Schooling can be another challenge. Again, global companies are going to encourage them to look at international schooling options. Depending on the age of their children, it may be the only way to go. It is hard for a child to move into a new culture when they are older and to be able to stay up to standard academically with the national school system.

However, the national school system is a great way to connect with the community from a strategic perspective and it also gives your child the language to thrive in the national culture. There are obvious exceptions and challenges to this. I do not recommend national schools all of the time, but if they start young, it can be a very rewarding experience. In Europe, for example, the national schools have good to excellent standards and can truly be beneficial for the child's development. Our children went to national schools for five years and, though challenging at times, it was worth it.

National schools may not always be an option. If the workers have children, this is a key question they will have. Since you are a person who lives there, you can walk them through the options and the pros and cons of each option.

Being ready, able, and also willing to engage in a dialogue about these items will be extremely helpful. This will often take a different way of relating to the marketspace worker. They will not be coming through normal mission organizational channels, therefore the manner in which you relate to them is important. In these cases, it is not about dictating their options, but conversing with them. You can help them think through the pros and cons, see their options, and think strategically about some of these logistical choices. This can make all the difference in the world for strategic engagement.

Not only do we as missionaries need to help with logistical matters in their arrival, we also need to think about some other ways in which we lead this type of worker.

EMPOWER AND RELEASE THEM TO LIVE STRATEGICALLY

I mentioned before about how our team changed from being a vocational missionary team to being a team largely composed of expat marketspace men and women who lived and worked in our city. I had to learn not only how to empower and equip them in this type of ministry, but also release them to do it.

Several years ago, I met each month with this group of marketspace professionals in Madrid. We loved those long Spanish lunches. A lunch hour is actually 2.5 hours at times, so I guess that could not technically be called a lunch hour! I saw this small group of men and women as my marketspace team. We went to different churches, we were involved in different communities, but we were trying to share the gospel with the people we were in contact with in our work and lives there.

We would pray together.

We would talk about our opportunities to share our faith.

We would talk about church.

We would talk about the challenges of being a believer there in the marketspace.

We would celebrate with one another.

We would have community together.

They became an unofficial team ... or at least, a team that wasn't official in terms of how many missionaries view a team. These men and women worked 50-plus hours a week in their regular jobs. Most of them were married with children. They had challenges of living abroad. They needed the community. They needed the encouragement. They needed the coaching. In many cases, they really just needed to be empowered with the knowledge that they are also sent ones and they can make a difference, even if they are not full-time vocational missionaries. They just needed to be released to do the work. Our group was able to provide some of that for them.

Despite these clear benefits, there are a few things you, as a missionary, should consider when adding marketspace workers who have regular jobs into your team.

SET PROPER EXPECTATIONS

Unclear expectations from team members or team leaders can lead to major conflicts on the field. I've worked with hundreds of teams over the years, and have seen this happen over and over. As a team leader, we have one expectation and the team member may have another expectation altogether.

Sometimes this is played out in your strategy, while other times it comes to light in community within the team. If the team member comes from a church that highly values living out faith through relationships, but the team leader has a strategy that is focused more on first encounter evangelism (sharing your faith the first time you have a conversation with someone), then you could have a potential problem.

If your team member has the expectation that you will meet all of his or her needs for friendship, but it is not realistic due to your ongoing ministry or season of life, then community could be on shaky ground.

If you as a team leader are expecting them to be able to work 40 hours a week like you do on "ministry stuff," but their workload will not allow that (or it isn't good for their family), then you will have differing expectations that could lead to conflict.

DEFINE THEIR ROLES

When you bring a marketspace worker into your team,

you should consider what type of role they will play. Often, business people are trained to be production oriented, expecting tangible results. We, as missionaries, usually like to live in ambiguity. We can love the vagueness of missionary life too much. Our schedules are super flexible. We can move in and out of roles on our team. The more you can identify what role they can play on the team and give them specific responsibilities or even estimates of the amount of time expected to fulfill that role, then you will be better off and everyone will be more productive.

Take some time on the front end and write out some roles you could fill on your team. As you talk with potential marketspace teammates, present those roles to them. Discover their areas of giftedness and passion. Chemistry is important for this type of teammate as well. You really do need good chemistry. You might find out early that they would not be a good fit for your team. If this is the case, then the best thing you can do is to encourage them, bless them, and pray for them, but decide that partnering with them at a deeper level is not the best path forward. You are a lot better off acknowledging this on the front end, rather than later on if they join the team.

MARKETSPACE WORKER ASSESSMENT

Many sending churches and missions organizations have what is called an assessment of the candidates that are going into vocational missionary work. While the assessment of the marketspace worker may look different, it is no less important. Even though they are not full-time team members, it is of paramount importance that the church and missionary team have confidence in who they are working with. It is vital to look for certain things for our teammates. As you assess potential marketspace people for your teams, keep these things in mind. What do you want to see them demonstrate in their lives overseas and on your team? Consider this list:

- A passionate follower of Jesus Christ
- Calling: if married, a sense of calling together for this type of work
- If married, a strong bond of love for one another
- If a parent, a commitment to love and nurture their children
- Adaptability: can they adapt to a variety of situations?
- Flexibility: are they flexible with their plans?
- Humility: do they demonstrate a humble spirit?
- Initiator: are they a self starter?
- Knows and understands their limits (capacity, responsibilities, balance of life, work, and ministry)
- Teachability: an avid learner
- Servant spirit: eager to serve
- Team player: willing to serve under a team leader
- Knows their own spiritual gifts and skills

After a person is assessed by the church, then the church can develop a one-page development plan to help the worker prepare for what is necessary to go overseas. Traditionally, for vocational missionaries this process of assessment, development, raising support, and going through a sending organization can take up to two years. This is the normal process.

HELIPAD SENDING

When sending marketspace workers, I believe the church has to think more in terms of developing a helipad rather than a runway. In the traditional sending mechanism that the church has used for years is to send out a vocational missionary. It often takes 12 to 18 months for that person or family to go through the process with the church, sending organization and raising support before they can leave for the field. This provides a lengthy runway for the church and organization to help prepare the missionaries for their move overseas. However, we have found with marketplace workers that they often get a job overseas and can be gone in a matter of one to three months. It looks more like a helipad where a helicopter can take off quickly.

The person who is awakened to take their job overseas could actually be able to get a job quickly, especially if they are a proven worker in their company and they talk to the human resource department and are given the green light for a job overseas. I have seen this more in the U.S. job market with people desiring to move across the country to be with a church plant. They talk to their department and suddenly find themselves with a new job role in that city in a moment's notice.

How can we help prepare marketspace workers to be ready? If the sending church is already considering this as a viable pathway, then they have a sending pipeline in place and are doing a lot of training and discipling naturally as a part of their church. So whether they embark on a traditional pathway that gives them

HOW CAN WE HELP PREPARE MARKETSPACE WORKERS TO BE READY?

a lot of time to prepare, or they are able to take off quickly, they are ready.

When putting together a development plan, it could be helpful to consider the following development categories: They first look at the **head**. What are the knowledge components this person needs to learn or grasp (theology, missiology, ecclesiology)? Secondly, what are the **heart issues** that need to be addressed (their marriage, soul care, walk with God, character flaws)? Lastly, what are the **missional skills** they need to learn to help them engage well overseas (sharing their faith story, looking for a person of peace, mapping, developing relationships)? We provide a lot of these skill pieces in our book, *Tradecraft: for the Church on Mission.*

BEWARE CONTROL ISSUES

Oh, how we like to control! We'd never admit it, but sometimes we can be control freaks. We struggle to maintain order by using our power of control. With full-time teammates who are part of your mission, you are able to have more of that control. You can set the schedule of where to meet and when to meet.

When workers have a regular job, it can be much more difficult. We are used to customizing the rules based on full-time teammates, but we have to change this if we are going to be able to see fruitful teams composed of expats who want to live intentionally.

Leadership is influence! You will have to lead this type of teammate from more of a relational aspect than a positional one. We are accustomed to leading positionally and often do not take into account the importance of relating to a person and being able to influence them through relationships.

INTEGRATING THEM INTO THE TEAM

One of the main sticking points for people coming over to live and work intentionally in another culture is that we don't know how to help them feel part of the team. Integration into a team is often complicated and it takes some work on the part of the full-time team to be able to do this well.

We are not accustomed to part-time workers. We often compartmentalize ministry and feel that they cannot be doing the "main thing" all of the time, so we label them second-class missionaries. We need to see them as an important part of the team. We need to have an integration plan for this type of worker. There are a few things to think about as you do this. We use these systems as we work with sending churches and missions organizations to prepare their workers to integrate new members into their team.

When they arrive, I recommend developing a 90-day plan that helps incorporate them into the team. It may mean that you have to change your meeting time. They will not be able to be at your 9 a.m. meetings during the work week. You may need to meet after they get off work or on the weekend. They cannot participate in every project or program your team has, but you can communicate well to them and give them tasks to perform to feel part of the team.

You should also include some reading in your 90 day on-ramping plan that will help them learn more about their new culture and some homework assignments to help them assimilate.

You should consider advising them to become familiar with your team values, vision, and strategy, so they can be on the same page as you when you have your team talk. If you use a lot of mission words and acronyms like missions organizations like to do, you will need to define those words. If you have them in print, even better.

Find ways to communicate with them on a regular basis. If you have a messaging system through text or chat, be sure to include them. Check in with them often in these first days. Invite them over for coffee or dinner. Take them to some outings in your city. Get to know the entire family as you would a full-time teammate.

I like teams who put together a team covenant for all members. The more you can communicate up front what you value, what your vision and strategy is, how you go about implementing your strategy, and what role each person plays, it will keep everyone on the same page.

PROCESS FOR INTEGRATING NEW TEAM MEMBERS

Here are some items to consider as you develop a process for this type of worker:

1. Think through the roles you have on your team that could be a good fit for a marketspace worker. Remember the more specific you can be in knowing what you need for them to do, the easier it should be to find the person that fits your team. They will also be able to know on the front end what they would be expected to do.
2. Think about what it will take language-wise for the gospel to move forward in this culture and how much language these workers need to be able to evangelize and disciple. And, before you start thinking they cannot do this because they do not know the language, don't forget that you didn't know the language at first, either. It *is* possible. With encouragement and some help, they can learn the language in this new setting.

3. Write out the skills necessary to learn to be a vital part of ministry in this city and how you can equip them.
4. Use Upstream's checklist from my book, *First 30 Daze: Practical Encouragement for Living Abroad Intentionally* (see Appendix).
5. Develop a 90 day pre-boarding document that will help you and them prepare for their arrival.
6. Have a 90 day on-ramping plan for how they can get started well.

CONFLICT

Unfortunately, conflict has been a part of missionary life since the beginning. It is obvious that the apostle Paul encountered some conflict along the way. Look at these words from Acts 15:36-41:

"And after some days Paul said to Barnabas, "Let us return and visit the brothers in every city where we proclaimed the word of the Lord, and see how they are." Now Barnabas wanted to take with them John called Mark. But Paul thought best not to take with them one who had withdrawn from them in Pamphylia and had not gone with them to the work. And there arose a sharp disagreement, so that they separated from each other. Barnabas took Mark with him and sailed away to Cyprus, but Paul chose Silas and departed, having been commended by the brothers to the grace of the Lord."

Paul and Barnabas had a falling out. These are the two that you can read about in Acts 13 when the church of

Antioch sent them out. They were long-term partners and friends. When the church of Antioch was being evaluated by the church leaders of Jerusalem in Acts 11, we see that the church trusted Barnabas and wanted him to go check this new church out. Barnabas went. He thought so much of Paul (called Saul at that time) that he went to find him and brought him back to be a part of this new church. But in Acts 15, we see these two had a sharp disagreement and it had to do with John Mark who had abandoned the work before. Barnabas wanted him on the team. Paul did not. They split ways. The good news of this relational journey is that in Galatians 2:1, we see where they again worked together. Paul even came to agree with Barnabas about the value of John Mark. See 2 Timothy 4:11. We do not have the inside story to all that brought the reconciliation about, but it seems evident that they made amends and started to work together again.

While we read that it happens, we should not just assume that it is natural. In many cases it can be avoided, but at times it cannot. When it cannot be avoided, you would do well to have a conflict plan for your team. I should be clear on this. I am not advocating that you need to have a plan to have conflict. I am advocating that you have a plan to move through the conflict in a way that honors Christ.

In some cases, you may have to part ways, but only after reconciliation has failed. If you encounter conflict, then what are some steps you can take toward resolving the conflict? Listen to one another. Keep trying to talk it out. Pray for one another. If necessary, bring in a third party to help you work through the issues. And did I mention pray for one another?

HOW THE CHURCH CAN PREPARE

The sending church is an important part of the equation of successful marketspace work. Since you see these members living, studying or working overseas as a viable expression of ministry, there are certain ways you can prepare and support them.

First and foremost, pray for them and their family. Just as you would with your vocational missionaries, find ways to pray for them as a mission team and as a church.

Provide care for them just as you would with your other missionaries. If your church has an advocate team or a missionary care team, be sure they are also covered.

Missionary Skills Training: Try to facilitate for them a weekend or week experience to learn missionary skills and strategy. There are several organizations that do this during different times of the year, including the organization I work with: The Upstream Collective. Upstream's "How to Think & Act Like a Missionary" event trains attendees to think and act like missionaries in their own contexts. Often, people are not able to go to a four-week training due to their work. Maybe you could help fund this training for them since they are not normally raising financial support.

Discipleship Training: If you have created a pipeline for this type of worker in your church, think through a plan in which you prepare and develop them. I think missionary skills are a normal part of discipleship since we see all through Scripture our responsibility in taking the gospel to the nations.

Language Learning: This is another important area for the worker as they arrive on the field. Most missions organizations and teams can help them find the right language plan. Some global companies in management positions actually offer tutoring or language classes as part of their package. But many people do not have that option and could use some help learning the language. It is not cheap in most places, and many missionaries do not normally raise support for this. The church can really step in and help provide some resources to help.

Send Them Off Well: Just as you often have commissioning services for your sent ones, be sure to find a way to do something similar. It may not be a public service or as formal due to security reasons, but you can pray for them as elders, missions teams, small groups, etc., and send them off well.

HOW THE MARKETSPACE WORKER CAN PREPARE

Take the initiative. This is a new and alternative pathway for most missions organizations and churches. It is, in many ways, uncharted waters for all parties involved. It will take you stepping out and asking questions, finding out information on your own, and often doing some of the work that traditionally may have been done by the church or missions organization. I think systems will evolve in the coming years as this is developed, but in missions work in general we have to create a lot of things from nothing.

Own your responsibility. At the end of the day, it is up to you and, if you are married, your family moving overseas. I think we often have this idea that items are checked off the list for us with our church or missions organization. This will not always be the case. Own the responsibility of your move and be proactive.

Ask to be assessed and developed by your church. The church knows you best, or at least they should. You have actively worshipped, served, and been a part of community. They can help you see your weaknesses. We all have them. We are not perfect people and no vocational missionary goes overseas as the perfect and complete worker. We all need developing. The church is in the best position to help you grow and mature as a Christ follower and in your missionary skills. Learning missionary skills of proclaiming the gospel and making disciples really is a natural part of every believer's discipleship.

HOW THE MISSIONARY CAN PREPARE

Andrew is a mechanical engineer. His company, based in the States, relocated him to a Western European country. He did not know anyone in the country. He was introduced to a full-time Christian worker who lived in a city about 50 miles from where he was being transferred. The mission strategist did not have any team members in that city, but he did know of a national church planter who was in the early stages of planting a church there. This guy was able to give a strategic introduction to the engineer. The first weekend he and his family were in their city, they were able to go to a BBQ for the church-planting team. They have been involved in church planting from the day they arrived in their new country.

A key person in the above scenario was what I call "The Connectionist." Sure, it sounds like the title of a Hollywood film. It isn't a real word, but it is essentially the person who connects the transnational marketspace worker with a viable ministry setting. There are some people who are naturally gifted at this. It is uncanny how a true connector just simply knows who is out there and how to connect them.

Tom Rath came out with a book quite a few years ago that has helped people discover their strengths. His reasoning is that we spend far too much time trying to perfect our weaknesses, and do not nurture our natural strengths. In his book called, *StrengthsFinder 2.0*, he lists 30 strengths people can have. I would recommend this book to anyone, but especially those who are considering working the marketspace abroad. Knowing how God has gifted you will greatly benefit and encourage you as you seek to live intentionally abroad.

However, I'm really telling you about this book

because one of the strengths a person can have is called "connectedness."

To be honest, I am one of these people. I do not totally understand what happens in my head. Sometimes, I feel it is just part of a giftedness that God has given me. When I start to get to know someone, I just sort of have an intuition of where they would be a good fit and who the next person is that they should talk with. Notice that I did not say I have the answers. I seldom do. It may not be their final step they need to take, but it can be a good connection.

I am looking for people like this all over the world. What if we built a network of connectionists that think the same way and can instantly connect people strategically everywhere in the world? It is important to have connectionists in most major cities. This is helpful so they can concentrate on a certain area or region of the world. It is rare that someone has connections everywhere in the world.

Here are some important aspects of a connectionist:

- They know their city well.
- They know the companies in their city.
- They even know the multinational companies of their city.
- They know the ministries operating in their city.
- They know the national churches.
- They know the local nonprofits.
- They know key leaders and influencers.

- They understand the needs of the city.
- They know the networks of the city and how to communicate within them.
- They are usually two or three introductions away from most people in the city.

The more and more I talk with people like this, the less I am convinced this is a learned trait. I am sure people would take me to task on this, but I do not know many people who set out to be connectors. They usually just are. In fact, I have found from experience when a person becomes an official connector, they often lose their full powers of connections. It sounds more like a superhero, but there is not a lot of profit in connecting. I haven't found people willing to pay for this service. Normally, you just make a strategic introduction and move on. If this becomes too institutionalized, it can become less effective. It needs to happen in a natural environment.

The Upstream Collective has quite a few members who are in various parts of the world through some sort of a missions or ministry organization. We have people who are in the marketspace, wanting to make strategic connections with our on-the-ground crowd and facilitate strategies for reaching neighborhoods or cities. These connectionists can: suggest neighborhoods that could be strategic to live in; connect them with ministries on the ground; coach them on the cultural adaptation; bring them on to be part of their team, even though it will be on a part-time basis; etc.

Be on the lookout for jobs and multinational companies.

Backtrack to where those companies are headquartered in the States and make contact with church leaders in those cities or areas near the company. You may just find a kingdom-minded professional who would be a person of influence to help direct Christ followers overseas.

PART FOUR: CREATING A COMMUNITY FOR YOU TO THRIVE IN

Moving overseas is like hitting the reset button on your life. You find yourself dropped into another culture, with another language, unknown social etiquette, and unfamiliar faces. Community can be the glue that bonds you to your new place in life. It provides that staying power that you will need. In community, we can celebrate with one another, grieve together, share life experiences and circumstances, and partake in each other's struggles and victories. It helps us not only to connect better to the new city and place we are living, but also helps us have a deeper sense of purpose in what we are doing.

Vocational missionaries, who are usually part of a larger team of missionaries in their own organization, are often grafted into a missionary community. Marketspace workers or students: you may also find community in your work or studies, but will you need something more?

In this chapter, I want us to look at various places where one can find community. When I think back over the 15 years that we worked overseas, community came about in different ways for us and from different groups throughout our time. All of them were helpful and they often happened simultaneously.

YOUR FAMILY

For some of you, you are moving overseas with a spouse and children. Others of you are single. There is no wrong answer here or better way. Both can work well in a variety of contexts. We moved over with two children. I will say, looking back, that it was living overseas that gave us a deep sense of belonging with one another as a family. It may have been the way in which people sat at the dinner table for a couple of hours talking that helped, but even to this day we love sharing meals with one another. We tend to have some of our deepest conversations around the table. I am not a natural game lover, but for whatever reason, we loved sitting down and playing board games or even working a puzzle while we were overseas. We also tried to be very sensitive about inviting singles who were on our team or who lived in our city to hang out at our house. We even would invite them to holiday functions when they did not have a family nearby. While your family will not be your only source for community, it can be a significant one.

YOUR NEIGHBORS

When we first moved overseas, we had no clue where to live. We basically started from scratch. Some of our colleagues suggested we live in a certain part of our city, so we looked there and found a place that met our family's needs. It was not a large apartment, but it had sufficient space for our small family. It was in a good location for our work. It was next to a park and we loved that for our children. What we had no idea about was the people who lived there. We were the only Americans who lived in our building. No one in our building knew English, so we were at their mercy. They showed us a lot of grace.

We were surprised to discover that the place was full of young families who had children the same ages as ours. The building had a fenced-in garden in the middle where everyone played. It was not long before we started making friends and people started inviting us to have coffee or dinner, and we in turn did the same. Our kids connected well with the people there, although not without normal kid conflict (like kicking the soccer ball over the fence). Actually, that was probably me. I am not the best soccer player.

I remember one time we had a plumbing problem and, instead of calling our American friends who lived about ten minutes away, I went upstairs. Initially, I faltered my way through in Spanish, but I didn't know the technical plumbing terms. So I got the guy to come downstairs and then I was able to point and grunt my way through the conversation. He made the call to a plumber who fixed the problem for us. This problem actually endeared us to our neighbors. Instead of looking for the answer on Google or calling a friend, we did our best to always seek out our neighbor.

Our neighbors became very close to us over the years. When the Madrid train bombings occurred in 2004, we took roses and a card to each family who lived in our building to show our sympathy and told them we were praying for their city and nation who came under attack. Even years after we moved out of the building, we still keep up, thanks to social media. When we visit Spain, we almost always reconnect with some of them.

They provided us with community. They were family to us when we did not have family here. We were fortunate ... it doesn't always happen that way in an apartment building. We have never seen it like that before or after. In some cases, it may just be one or two of your neighbors, but my encouragement to you is to try to connect with them. Seek out your neighbors to be part of your community.

YOUR WORK COLLEAGUES

For many of you, your day will be in the office or building where you work. In many cultures outside the U.S., work colleagues can provide a strong sense of community. Work colleagues often get together for social times after work or even on weekends. Building and obtaining community with your workmates can be tricky. They may or may not be receptive to outsiders. I have found from my other expat friends that if you work hard at learning the language, enjoy their culture, become a learner, and even take the initiative to go out for coffee or lunch, they may be more open.

YOUR GROUPS

Another place you can find community is based around your hobbies or your children's hobbies. Our children were always involved in music lessons or sports clubs. We also played sports and we found that having these hobbies can provide places to connect and grow deeper in natural relationships around the activity. When you play or participate in a group week after week, you begin to get to know people and relationships can be formed. We will discuss hobbies more later, but if you already have a hobby, why not try to find some groups that also enjoy the same hobby when you move overseas? There is no need to work all the time. Enjoy the things you like to do, and along the way, I bet you will meet others who do also. This will create a valuable sense of community in your life.

YOUR CHURCH

Being connected to the local church may not seem like an easy task, and often, it's not. But it is a great place for you to be in community with other believers. Each person living overseas needs to decide for themselves where God would have them get involved. For some, that means getting plugged into an international church and serving there. In Europe, we've seen an increase in the number of Europeans who want to attend international churches, regardless of their religious affiliation.

If language is a hard thing for someone, or their job

requires them to mainly function in English, they can find opportunities to engage peoples from all over the world and even their new home culture if they attend a local international church.

However, there are so many advantages to being involved in a local church led by nationals. If you've ever sat in a church service that does not use English, you know that within a few minutes, you may feel overwhelmed, lost, and by the time you get home, you are probably exhausted. **But the blessings of attending a national church are endless!** First, it puts you in a position of humility. You are their guest. You need their help in understanding what is being said. You may not even be able to serve that much due to your language abilities, and in fact, may find them serving you! What a great lesson in humility.

Second, the local church usually knows far more than you do about the nuances of their culture, and how the gospel can be communicated in a way that is relevant. If a marketspace worker would get involved in a local church, they are sure to find many natural ways to connect with fellow believers and learn how they can best relate to their unbelieving co-workers. It is definitely not the easiest route to take, in terms of finding fellowship, but we believe God is thrilled when someone is willing to step out of their comfort zone and partner with believers from another culture.

But perhaps most importantly, your local church can give you a great sense of belonging and rootedness. It provides much-needed community. It grounds you in the culture. It encourages you to have other local believers investing in your life.

Just as important as it is to have a sending church back in the States (or your home country), it is also important to have a faith community to connect with while you are overseas. One needs a local church where they are living to give them a place to worship, serve, be discipled, be shepherded, have biblical community, etc.

YOUR MISSIONARY TEAM

I am a proponent of joining a missionary team or strategic activity that can give you missional focus. This can come from your local church, or it could be a local team that is focusing on a particular work strategy. This could be another non-profit or it could be a missionary team from a missions organization. This team can provide you with a sense of focus and clarity on why you are there. It can give you a sense of community to be connected with like-minded men and women who want to see kingdom work advance. Every team that I have been a part of has been a source of community for us. Sure, we focus on work, but we also hang out with one another and do life with one another as opportunity arises. This type of community often provides you with a deeper purpose for your being there.

FINDING COMMUNITY

When the Lord started to lead me and my family toward overseas missions, I began having some of the same thoughts as you. I am just a normal, American guy, who has a heart for God and I want to follow him and tell others about Jesus. How would I be received in another country?

I remember talking about this as a family before we moved to Madrid in 2001. We felt there were several things that would help us connect with the culture there — but we knew being an American would not be one of them.

As we entered into this new culture, we always tried to be aware of three things:

1. Make eye contact and smile.
2. Try our best to speak the language of our new culture — to make an effort, even if it was only a word or two. People appreciate the effort, even if the sentence is grammatically incorrect.
3. Be humble. I must admit being humble was not a hard thing to do once I tried number two on the list; five year olds would remind me how badly I spoke! But many people naturally think Americans are loud and arrogant. We wanted to break that stereotype and at the same time reflect the attitude of Christ.

By practicing these elements, we were received well into community. It was not always easy and automatic. It took time and often our community looked very different from place to place. However, we were able to enter into relationships. We made friends. We became part of their community. We had opportunities to share the gospel with our words and our lives. This was exactly why we moved overseas!

PART FIVE: STRATEGIC FOCUS

THE MARKETSPACE WORKER NEEDS TO SEIZE OPPORTUNITIES

In the book *Tradecraft: For the Church on Mission*, we wrote about missionary skills that are important for all believers to practice. We believe these skills are a normal part of our growth as a disciple. In this section, we will investigate some important missional behaviors that will help you as you try to strategically engage with those in your new city.

As we look at engaging these people where we live, one of the first things we need to do is to have a complete reliance on the Holy Spirit. The Holy Spirit not only convicts us of sin, gives us courage, and comforts us, but he also provides guidance in mission. Another aspect to consider is what Caleb Crider calls, "the geometry of disciple making."[11]

PERPENDICULAR AND PARALLEL (+ / =)

As we go about our days and weeks, interacting with people, we tend to have perpendicular (+) or parallel (=) paths. How can we live in a constant response to the Holy

11 Crider, Caleb. Tradecraft.

141

Spirit's guidance for opportunities to proclaim the gospel and serve people?

PERPENDICULAR PATHS

There is an important aspect of living by the Spirit on mission. I call this "being invited in." Perhaps one of the most concrete examples of being led by the Spirit comes from the story of Philip and the Ethiopian official in Acts 8:

"As for Philip, an angel of the Lord said to him, 'Go south down the desert road that runs from Jerusalem to Gaza.' So he started out, and he met the treasurer of Ethiopia, a eunuch of great authority under the Kandake, the queen of Ethiopia. The eunuch had gone to Jerusalem to worship, and he was now returning. Seated in his carriage, he was reading aloud from the book of the prophet Isaiah. The Holy Spirit said to Philip, 'Go over and walk along beside the carriage.' Philip ran over and heard the man reading from the prophet Isaiah. Philip asked, 'Do you understand what you are reading?' The man replied, 'How can I, unless someone instructs me?' And he urged Philip to come up into the carriage and sit with him" (Acts 8:26-31).

I love this story. I pray my life will be as fine-tuned as that. Here we have a preacher who, instead of being led to the city, was led to go on a road away from town. He was on the south road. I get this picture of a man walking (Philip) and a man riding (the Ethiopian official). So the Spirit tells Philip "go walk beside the chariot."

Philip must have been in shape enough to do it. I think my tendency would have been to go over and ask for a ride, but the Bible tells us that Philip ran over there. Actually, one of my good friends mentioned that it would be often common in that day to travel with a group of people. His carriage could be one of several in the group. It probably was not that uncommon for people to walk along with the group and for beggars to come up and ask for favors. Many people wanted to get a look — after all, this was an important man.

Philip's mindset was different. He had a specific direction. The Holy Spirit led him to go south out of Jerusalem and toward Gaza. This could have been hard for Philip. He was being led in a direction away from the city where the church began. The church was being spread out and dispersed.

The story concludes with the Ethiopian coming to faith in Christ. I think the obedience that Philip had in following the leadership of the Holy Spirit was crucial. The Spirit provided the opportunity for the gospel to be explained to this man in a way in which he could understand and ultimately accept.

There are at least two important points to this passage:

1. Be sensitive to the Holy Spirit's leading
2. Be obedient to the Holy Spirit once he leads

Philip did both and we can learn from this. As Philip obeyed the Spirit and went to the chariot, he overheard the Ethiopian official reading. Making the most of this divine

THE MARKETSPACE

opportunity, he asked if the man understood what he was reading. He was then invited into the life of this Ethiopian official. Philip told him the good news, starting with Isaiah 53:7-8. The official asked Philip to baptize him. For us to be like Philip, this requires the Spirit's guidance. It requires our obedience and preparation.

How does this affect us as we live our lives on mission everyday? How does this apply to a church as it lives out the Great Commission? How can this apply to missions organizations or church planting teams who sometimes have long-term strategy plans? Perhaps I look at my own circumstances to determine the direction of the Lord.

HOW DOES THIS AFFECT US AS WE LIVE OUR LIVES ON MISSION EVERYDAY?

But I believe that as we consistently seek the Lord through prayer and the Scriptures, we will understand his will for us. I believe this applies to all areas of our lives.

We often base a lot of our evangelism efforts on perpendicular paths. We pray for opportunities to share our faith with a stranger that sits next to us or the person on the plane. We look for those divine appointments. And very often, God gives them to us.

Are we ready? Are we open?

PARALLEL PATHS

Parallel paths deliberately model for someone what it would look like for someone from their culture to follow Jesus. This is our everyday life. This is being what Jesus described as salt and light in Matthew 5. This is living out your faith wherever you live, work, and play. Think about Jesus and the calling of the twelve disciples:

"As Jesus was walking beside the Sea of Galilee, he saw two brothers, Simon called Peter and his brother Andrew. They were casting a net into the lake, for they were fishermen. 'Come, follow me,' Jesus said, 'and I will send you out to fish for people.' At once they left their nets and followed him. Going on from there, he saw two other brothers, James son of Zebedee and his brother John. They were in a boat with their father Zebedee, preparing their nets. Jesus called them, and immediately they left the boat and their father and followed him" (Matthew 4:18-22).

Jesus invites Peter and Andrew to follow Him. There is not a gospel presentation here, or at least how evangelicals define one. In this case, the gospel is Jesus, himself. He simply says "follow me." The fishermen drop their nets and follow Jesus. The men spend three years being discipled by Jesus. The disciples minister alongside Jesus. Confession and belief is a part of their growth process. There is an ongoing, personal relationship. All through the gospel we see Jesus and the disciples living life together and intersecting and interacting with the people they encountered.

MAKING INTENTIONAL CHOICES

How do you intentionally engage the culture in which you have been placed? Famous missionary Jim Elliot once said, "Wherever you are, be all there." To me, this is an essential characteristic of a person seeking to live missionally.

So many times, we are everywhere except where we are in the present. We are dreaming about where we want to live or do ministry. Or we are back in Egypt, Spain, or fill in the blank. We think about how it was before. What happens is that we tend to cheat on our investment in the place where we are. What if you are only in a place for six months, 12 months, or three years? Does that affect the way you live your life? Some people would say yes. I am one of those people.

You may think that since you will be moving on shortly, there's little point in investing in someone. Instead, what if you made the most of every opportunity where you are planted today? Many of us have found ourselves living and working in Europe, Africa, or Asia, as well as many other places around the globe. Many have sensed a strong calling to come there and work. You may have been placed somewhere for a season, but you want to live missionally while you are there. Whatever the case, making intentional choices is where it begins. I think it is about making intentional choices to engage in the community and not just in the Christian (or American) subculture of that community, if there is one.

My wife, Susan, gave a terrific example of this while we were living in Spain. Shortly after we moved to Madrid in 2001, Susan was at an event at our children's school one morning, sitting with a group of Spanish mothers who also had kids at the school. She did not know a lot of Spanish, but she was trying. One of the mothers asked Susan, "You know that there is an American Women's Club here in Madrid, don't you?" Susan said, "Well, no, I did not, but besides — this is my community, and you all are my friends. I want to have Spanish friends." Susan was an instant hit. She had access to the community. She made an intentional choice to engage in the community. There is nothing wrong with the American Women's Club. They have some awesome events there in Madrid, as we later found out, but the point is that it was not Susan's default setting to choose the easy route. Her default setting was to intentionally immerse herself in the culture. It can be so easy for us to gravitate toward the familiar.

I know in the South, where I am from, the Christian subculture is so strong. When you move into a community, it's usually easy to find a really cool church of whatever style or flavor you want, and you can start developing community with the people in that church ... and never meet **WE MAKE CHOICES TO ENGAGE OR DISENGAGE EVERY DAY.** anyone in your own neighborhood. It does not have to be that way, but it is that easy. We make choices to engage or disengage every day.

One of my mentors who has shaped my missional think-ing over the years is a guy by the name of Lonnie Reynolds. Lonnie and I are both on the leadership side of our organi-zation, and so we could sit in front of the computer all day long and never interact with anyone else. Lonnie was telling me the other day that he likes to do his administration stuff in the morning so that in the afternoon and evening he can go into his community and hang out with people. He has taught me strategies for gospel interaction. But the last thing I want to do is prescribe a certain method or program. About the time a formula starts working, circumstances change anyway — not to mention that my culture here will look different from where you live. For me, I have to intentionally choose to leave the computer and get out of my house if I am going to be missional.

Think about the intentional choices or opportunities that you have when you move to a new place.

- Where do you live?
- If you have children, where do they go to school?
- What clubs are there to join?
- What hobbies do you have? Are they individual hob-bies, or do they allow you to be in community with others?
- Where do you shop?
- Do you directly deposit checks through your iPhone, or do you go inside the bank so you can have a

conversation?

- Where do you go for your neighborhood coffee or tea?
- Do you look on social media to find a new restaurant or download a map app to get directions, or do you stop and ask a local?
- Where do people normally hang out?

Of course, this list is not exhaustive, but you get the idea. We make choices about how we engage the community where we live.

GIVING AND RECEIVING HOSPITALITY

When we close the doors of our homes, we close the doors of our hearts. Debra Hirsch

Living in another country is hard. Working within another culture's ideologies is hard. At the end of the day, most expats just want to be home. It's their haven for speaking English, eating comfort food, and a way to shut out the realities of living overseas.

When we think about the Jesus we say we follow, we have to imagine what a day of work must have looked like for him. Everyday, he spent time with people who misunderstood who he was, what he was saying and what he stood for. Many of the people he came into contact with couldn't care less about getting to know him as a person. If you are an expat reading this, you can probably relate.

We have to remember that when Jesus came to earth to live among us, he stepped out of his own comfort zone. He went from a perfect world, living with his father, to become a lowly human being. Talk about a cross-cultural leap! Yet we see in the Bible that Jesus was the epitome of hospitality — both giving it and accepting it. We need to follow his example.

Hospitality is huge when you live overseas. Yes, your home can be a much-needed sanctuary for you, but it's also a place that you can welcome people in. Show them you care enough to cook them a meal, share a coffee, and listen to their life stories. Be willing to open up your home to your neighbors. It may just be a quick, informal visit as you ask them a question about utilizing a Spanish appliance, but even that will build bridges with your neighbors.

What about receiving hospitality? Other cultures seem to be so much better at this than we are. If someone invites you to their home, say yes! Sure, you will probably spend a lot of the time feeling out of place, lost in conversation (if you are speaking in the native tongue) and if the food is still something you are getting used to, then you may find yourself graciously choking down a piece of meat. But don't miss the blessing of receiving hospitality from a neighbor. It will build strong connections for your relationship that hopefully lead to conversations about the God you serve.

A few years ago, Susan and I had the opportunity to visit a city in the Middle East, where there were many Syrian refugees seeking a new home. We went with another humanitarian aid worker to visit a new arrival. This woman, her children, her sister's family, and her mother all lived together. They shared a one-room apartment with a tiny kitchen just outside the only main room. It served as their bedroom and living room. Imagine 12 people living in the size of a small living room.

As we made our greetings and were welcomed into her apartment, she had us sit down around the edges of the wall where we all faced one another. She left the room for a few minutes and shortly returned with tea, plastic cups, and cookies. She had little, but wanted to demonstrate what was culturally appropriate for her, showing hospitality. It was extremely important that we received it well.

JOIN THE EXISTING

In my opinion, one key missional question is this: Do I create something from nothing, or do I join something that is already in existence? I have been faced with this question both in the North American context and in the European context. When I go into a new area to begin ministry, how do I connect with people?

One model is to start a ministry or group from scratch. You get to know your area. You determine certain needs and then you create something to meet that need. Maybe it is an English camp, food distribution, or a seeker Bible study. The idea here is to be able to create a group from nothing.

The simple strategy steps would be to:

- Determine needs
- Get a big idea
- Put your plan together to start the group
- Invite people to the group, either by word of mouth or other marketing strategies

But what if there is another way? What if the best way to enter into a culture would not be to start a group but to find a way to join an existing group? Instead of being the driver of a new ministry, what if you could connect even deeper by joining a group that is already in existence? In Europe, there are many different clubs in the community. What if you simply find a club that interests you and join it? You start getting to know the people. You have fun participating in the club. Pretty soon, you may be invited into some significant spiritual conversations. It's a win-win.

Sometimes we need to join an existing group. Be the learner, not the doer. I see this in a sense with Paul as he interacted in Athens. He was a tentmaker by trade. He went into the marketplace on a regular basis. We also know he was sharing his faith. The council in Athens invited him to speak to them and explain his "babblings." As Paul worked in the marketplace and was able to share his faith in the context of his work, he was likely invited into their place to share the gospel.

FIND A HOBBY

What do you like to do? Sometimes, we may make living as a missionary harder than it needs to be. Just be normal. Be an interesting person. As you do your hobby, you'll find some people who also like it. Live as a follower of Jesus in your new context. This may seem like a very simplistic idea, but finding a hobby that you actually enjoy doing is crucial to missional living in any culture.

It used to be that if you wanted to engage someone outside of your culture, you had to have some kind of outreach program that often included a spiritual tract or puppet show. These days, we know that people are willing and eager to interact with those who are different than they are if it's through a mutual interest.

If you enjoy playing a sport, find a way to do that in your host country. One young man loved to play soccer, so when he moved to Spain, he had a natural way to connect with other men in his neighborhood. After a few months of attending a Spanish church, he was invited to play soccer with men from the church. Instead of trying to create his own league or team, he joined something that already existed. This worked well because he had the opportunity to learn from the believers in his church as they all interacted with the guys from the neighborhood and unbelieving friends that came to play.

Meredith is a mom who really enjoys scrapbooking.

Although this is a concept that is very foreign to women outside of the U.S., she has found that women in her country love it. She has been able to do something that she loves alongside women from her culture and has built some great relationships through it. On multiple occasions, she has been able to share her faith and how it affects her daily life.

BE A LEARNER

Churches often ask what they can do on the mission field. How can they help? They commonly ask this, assuming the answer will be that they should come to teach, show, model, and develop the people they are trying to help. We come in as teachers. We come in as healthcare workers. We come as scientists. We come in as business leaders. And to be honest, sometimes we come across as know-it-alls.

What if, instead, we came in as learners? I had this idea a few years back when a church asked me if they could come over and put on a soccer camp for youth. I lived in Spain at the time — enough said! But instead of ending the conversation there, I decided I would toss out an idea. I suggested that instead of coming over to start up a soccer camp, why not come over and be part of an existing soccer camp? This way you would be learning with them. **The key is to come into a place and get to know people and be able to share the gospel in a relevant and relational way.** While this church decided not to pursue this route, other churches have moved toward the model of being learners. One church that meets in their own coffee shop decided to send a couple of their baristas to attend a barista school in Italy. Coffee not your thing? That's okay. Your creativity is the limit. In 2012, I led a trip to Tokyo with a group of pastors. We ate a lot of sushi, but we also met a lot of people living as salt and light in a difficult place. Here is an excerpt from my journal:

Yesterday in Tokyo, we met with a Japanese businessman. We were able to ask him a lot of questions. We learned a ton from this guy, but here is a good word that I wanted to share. When asked how can we prepare North American business people to come over and successfully work in an international setting, he said, "tell them to listen first." So many times we are known for speaking and telling others how to do things before we have any relational credibility established. He said we need to work hard in our jobs and we need to listen first. In his experience, once you do these two things, you will have an audience more interested to hear about your life or business suggestions. How well do I listen?

DEMONSTRATE PATIENCE

I always say that when you travel to another culture, you need to have humility and be a learner. Be willing to laugh at yourself as you make language mistakes and cultural blunders. You cannot be an instant success with language, work, and relationships when living overseas. It takes time, so give yourself some grace. Be patient with your family, and be patient with yourself as you practice the language, figure out public transportation, and learn the ins and outs of your new culture. I once heard that it takes six to seven years of living in a country before most people become truly fluent in another language. If this is the norm, try not to stress if language learning is slow.

I can speak from experience in this area. Learning Spanish was a task that proved somewhat difficult for me. I worked hard at it, and I attempted to use it as much as possible, but I was way behind my wife when it came to fluidity in conversation. There was no other choice but to be patient and trust that my language abilities would increase with time.

The ability to exhibit patience will get you very far in another country. Every time you find yourself waiting in a long line (or mob, in some countries) at the post office or some other place of business, try and forget you are on a time crunch. Most likely, you aren't as pressed for time as you'd think. If you are like me, it's in your nature to hurry and maximize your time. However, when waiting in a long line, see this as an opportunity to observe your culture. What are people doing while they wait their turn? How do they interact with each other? If you can practice patience, you may learn quite a bit about the people you've come to live among.

SHARE EXPERIENCES

Shared experiences can lead to spiritual conversations. I take the train into the city. In theory, it is an easy thing to do. I go to the station, buy a ticket, and get on the train. For some reason, the second step caused me problems in

Germany. Each time I went downtown, I had a problem with simply buying a ticket. If I could speak with a person, then I could make it happen. I could point and grunt and try to pronounce the words enough to get the ticket. But Germany is automated in many ways and you have to actually buy your ticket at an automated kiosk. Again, simple in theory, but you need for the machine to actually work. From my experience, there was usually only one of the machines that worked at any given station. There was one machine on each side of the tracks. I chose the wrong machine at least three times. However, I had the opportunity to have three conversations each time from some fellow strugglers who also had problems getting a ticket from the machine. Each time, the frustration of not being able to get a ticket when I wanted it led to a conversation with someone.

I wonder if such conversations have anything to do with a common experience. If a group of people who do not know each other are thrown together, say in an elevator, then it is quite normal for no conversations to take place unless the elevator becomes stuck. Then conversations would take place due to this common experience of crisis. There has to be a sociological term for this.

I found this crisis point quite helpful in trying to get a ticket at the rail station. One morning, there was a young lady who was also traveling to the city. I could not get a ticket from the right side of the track, so I did the proper thing and walked around to the crosswalk and across the tracks to the other side and purchased my ticket. This young woman who was on the other side of the tracks, still trying to convince the machine to work, saw that I had a ticket in hand, so she decided to come to my side. She did not have time to walk to the crossing, so she just jumped down and walked across the tracks (the picture I am painting is not that unsafe; we were in a small town, and at this point I was just trying to be culturally appropriate).

She came over to my side of the tracks. I walked around to the crosswalk and came back to the platform. She beat me there, of course, because she simply walked across the tracks. I saw some sign that vaguely resembled "high voltage," and felt walking was a better option. After we both had our tickets in hand, we decided we would try to talk. We were bonded by this experience. We started in German and she knew that was not going to get her far. I reluctantly tried Spanish, but she could not understand me completely. She was Romanian. So we settled on English. She began to tell me all about her German classes, getting a visa here to live, always having problems on this train, and so on. I thought about letting her know it would actually be better to use the crosswalk, but I decided against it. We talked for a while before the train arrived at the station and thus parted ways.

The very next time I went to the same station and tried to buy a ticket. This time I was in a hurry trying to catch the train. I went up to the kiosk and attempted to buy my ticket. It was not working, or I was not reading German correctly, and then I was bailed out by a businessman who lives in that area but commutes to Basel each morning. He told me that

I needed correct change, which I did not have and which he had. I think I paid a little more for my ticket that morning. He was a shrewd businessman. Once we got on the train, we were able to ride in together. He had an appointment. I did not get a phone number or business card, but we had a good conversation and he gave me some cultural pointers — like always carry change to buy your ticket.

My point in these stories is that a crisis (in these cases, even extremely minor ones) can often generate a great opportunity for conversations. You never know how the Lord can orchestrate such conversations. I am learning more and more to be sensitive to the Holy Spirit as he gives me these opportunities.

AS YOU GO

We read of the Great Commission from Jesus. Jesus gives us the command to make disciples. The command is not just to "go," but to make disciples ... disciples of the nations. As you read this passage, the Greek word "go," as it is used here, literally means "as you go." I think Jesus is assuming that as a follower of him you will go and tell people about Jesus. How can we be salt and light intentionally? Strategically?

We were overseas from 2001-2016. During the last few years, I began really thinking through the categories of how we engage people. These aren't abstract thoughts, but rather practical observations of my life in regards to strategically engaging not-yet believers with the gospel.

1. Sometimes we need to say something

My wife and I try to pray every morning. We find the morning the best time to do this as a couple. We share ways where we are salt and light and pray for people God puts in our pathways. To be honest, Susan has many more encounters. She is so in tune with the Lord.

Susan was telling me that she was in a store during Christmas time. At the checkout, she recognized that the cashier did not look like she felt well. Susan started talking with her and, sure enough, the girl was sick and just trying to make it through her shift. Susan wished her well and went on her way. As Susan left the store, the Holy Spirit prompted her to demonstrate kindness to this woman. She ran to Starbucks and grabbed a hot tea and brought it back to the cashier. The girl was blown away. She could not comprehend that a customer would serve her in that way.

But the Holy Spirit was not finished with the story. The Spirit prompted Susan not to just give something to her, which would have been fine. The Spirit prompted her to talk with her about the why. Susan was able to share the gospel with her. The cashier looked bewildered and said, "Some man came in yesterday and handed me this." She pulled out a token with the inscription, "Jesus loves you."

I wish I could tell you that she accepted the Lord and is a Christ follower. She has not at this point. But I believe God is trying to get her attention. We often feel we need to give the person all of the message at one time. Instead, we should be obedient to these seemingly small encounters where we share what we know and who we are and how God has changed our life. This is being salt and light in a very real way.

2. Sometimes we need to do something

I am talking about a random act of kindness. Most of the time, you know when you need to do something. As a follower of Jesus, you have the Holy Spirit living within you. The Holy Spirit gives you guidance as you live out your life on mission. For example, a friend mowed my lawn during a crazy, busy time twelve years ago. I still remember it.

Here are a few other examples of things you may feel led to do:

- Giving your lunch to a homeless person
- Holding the door open for someone when they are carrying an armload of stuff
- Picking up some extra work to help a coworker
- Reacting positively when someone is taking their bad day out on you
- Buying a cup of coffee for the person in line behind you at the coffee shop
- Mowing your neighbor's lawn or taking the garbage can out to the street

People take note of that. We can actually make a difference

in someone's life.

3. Sometimes we need to start something

Sometimes we have an idea and we need to run with it. In 2005, Madrid had one of the hottest, driest summers on record. We had a team there that worked with immigrants. They were suffering because most of them had to work the streets in the heat of the day. We contacted a humanitarian aid resource non profit with our idea and they gave us a large grant to buy a lot of bottles of water. We partnered with a group from Campus Crusade, which is now called CRU, and they provided us copies of *The Jesus Film*. We worked with some stateside churches to provide Bibles in various languages and we were set. We started the Living Water Project, where we gave out lots of water and some living water. We saw a need. We knew the Lord was speaking to us about a solution. We were obedient and he provided.

4. Sometimes we need to join something

A few years ago, I was in the Middle East. It was a fascinating time. One of the situations I was able to observe is the refugee crisis among Syrians. Syrians were pouring out of their country and into Iraq, Jordan, and Turkey. I was able to go by the U.N. refugee camp. You could not enter it, but you could get close enough to see. It was incredible. As large as it is, the truth is that it only contains about thirty percent of the refugees who are coming to these countries. The rest settle in cities and often the smaller ones near the border. So you can imagine if a city is built of 15,000 people but suddenly 25,000 people start living there ... their infrastructure is crushed. Schools stop working, garbage litters the streets, people and cars try to go down the same road, and living spaces become overcrowded.

A group of Christian business workers living near this city told me about a project that was going on to help these refugees. They would take water, food, and other things to help these families out. They decided that instead of trying to start their own project (as Americans, we like to do that), they would simply join an existing local one to give it more strength and long-term sustainability.

Now think about these four categories where you currently live. As a marketspace worker, you will most likely not be able to do everything. Just because you cannot give all of your time and attention to vocational ministry does not mean that you are a second-class missionary. You will have opportunities to engage people that I will never be able to meet. You will have the natural credibility with people by having a job with your company. Nonetheless, you will have to make choices in what you do and how you do it. I think these four categories can give you a simple grid of the type of work you do.

CHALLENGES FOR THE MARKETSPACE WORKER

Several challenges face the person who is intentionally

taking a job abroad to reach the nations. I would say there are two very broad and over-generalized categories of expat believers who have regular jobs overseas.

One category, which would probably be the largest, is believers whose current job is relocating them to another country. They want to live out their lives on mission, but they have not really had a choice where they land. I know that most marketspace workers are in this category. They work for "X" company. They are willing to move overseas to work internationally, but they have little choice as to where they live in the world or how long they will stay.

John worked for an international company in the green energy field and his company rather suddenly asked him to move to Europe. At first it was just for several months, but after three months, they told him they wanted him to live there for another nine months. John had a child in high school, and he and his wife had to decide whether or not they would be willing to move the entire family or simply enter a season of living separately but seeing each other once every other month.

In this case, since they had a high school child, they decided to simply let the husband work there and then find ways to see each other as a family every month or so. He contacted me to find out the best way to connect missionally while he lived in Europe. After talking through some of these challenges, we decided on a course of action where he locked arms with a local church that had a heart for the nations. He became a part of this church, which also provided him a good faith community and new friends in his new country.

One of the most helpful things a marketplace worker can do is to think and pray through these challenges and come up with a course of action that would help them live intentionally. I go back to the story of Paul in Acts 17 when he went to Athens. He was waiting for his co-workers who were traveling to him.

As I read this, I am struck that Paul did not idly wait around. He went to the marketplace where he knew he could connect with people. He went to the places of worship for the Jewish people, places where he knew people were thinking about God. He found ways to share the gospel where he was and not knowing how long he would actually be there. In so many cases, when we hit a transitory time, we shift into neutral and then six months, one year, or five go by. It is so important as sent out ones to live each day and each place with equal importance. Still, there are challenges. Let's take a look at them.

I. YOUR TIME (OR LACK THEREOF)

I work with quite a few missions organizations and talk with many full-time Christian workers who live overseas. One thing that comes up quite a bit in reference to marketspace workers is that they will not have time for the "main thing." When you hear this, they are saying the main thing is to do evangelism and discipleship. The theory of this is that when you work a full-time job 40-plus hours a week, you will not have time to do the "main thing" as other Christian workers can do.

This could be a compartmentalized view of mission. They see their life, their work, and their place as separate components. All of our life and all that we do blends together. Therefore, when you are at work, you have the opportunity to be in gospel conversations. You have the chance to disciple the people you are working with. Truthfully, I find myself as a full-time missionary sometimes very challenged to have moments to connect with people. **But our jobs themselves can help connect us with others.**

However, there is a flipside to this. The reality is that you will be working a lot as a marketspace professional. Unless you have created a pathway that gives you passive income to live on, then you will most likely work 40, 50, and even 60 hours a week, depending on your level of leadership or management in your company. Your company is not sending you to live overseas to have an easy job. They have extremely high expectations. So you do have a challenge in how you will spend your time. If you have a spouse and/or children, your free time is even more of a challenge.

Possible Solutions

Quite a few business people who are limited in the amount of time they have, can set aside a few hours each week to work on a tangible project. These could range from homework or tutoring help for children, teaching soft business skills, volunteering for projects in underserved areas, working with refugees, coaching sports, and so much more.

2. WHERE YOU LIVE

One of the choices you will have to make is where you live. In most large global cities, there are certain areas where internationals live. The international schools are located in these areas. They seem to be more open, which makes working and commuting easier. However, this may not be the best place for you to live in regards to mission.

Possible Solutions

Before you move, talk to people in your new city who can help you think through the most strategic place for you to be. If you need to live in an area that is better for your family in school, do not be discouraged. You might just need to spend a little more time in local travel so you can engage the people your team is seeking to reach.

3. PLUGGING INTO A FAITH COMMUNITY

You must be wondering how this could be a challenge. We really do need to be a part of a faith community — not only for fellowship with other believers, but also for our own soul care. In some cases, churches overseas are under-resourced, especially when you compare them to your previous church in the States. They lack people, leaders, finances, etc. While you have a heart to reach the nations, some of these churches can be stuck in a survival mode and they become possessive and want you to only work in the programs that they have. In some cases, these programs may reach out to the very people you want to connect with, but sometimes they don't. Unfortunately, I have seen some churches become possessive of their expat members, not wanting them to work in strategies they do not endorse.

Possible Solutions

Try to find faith communities that share the same or a similar vision to yours. I do not think they have to share every aspect of what you think is the perfect church for you and your family, but if they share a Great Commission vision, then you may be just the person they need to engage more people in their city. Personally, I have a list of churches I know, both national and international, that I can feel good about suggesting to expat marketplace workers.

4. ACCESS TO THE PEOPLE YOU WANT TO ENGAGE

I know a couple who works in a city where there are a lot of immigrants from hard-to-reach places. He works in a management role with their international company. When he took the job, he soon discovered he had no access to the immigrants he felt he was supposed to reach. He lived in their city, but the people he wanted to connect with did not work in the professional sector. He had lots of opportunities to share the gospel with nationals but not with immigrants.

Possible Solutions

One solution would be to live in an area populated by the people you are trying to reach. In this way as you go to the market, the park, school, etc., you are able to engage the people you want to connect with. Another solution is to find some partners and/or churches that reach out to these people. Join in on their teams and find ways to partner with them.

5. LEARNING THE LANGUAGE

You had to know I was going to get to this. You may be very good with languages. I am not. I have had to work extremely hard in my language learning skills. I am from East Tennessee, so even English is a second language for me (ha ha). However, to begin gospel conversations, which is the language of the heart, it is important to have language skills. Do not fret nor be looked down upon by full-time workers who have learned the language. They also started out at zero at some point. You can learn it, but you may have to work at it more intentionally since you have a full-time job.

Possible Solutions

Since you work in a company overseas, most likely they have hired people who are from that country, and thus speak the language. Learn from them. Talk to them. Spend time with them. Language will come.

Many companies offer language classes for their international workers. Be sure to ask for this as part of your moving package. Try to start every conversation in the local language. Even if you stink at it, do it. Stay in the conversation as long as you can. This will pay great benefits. **Let your new friends know you need to and want to learn the language.** In most cases, they will be very glad to help even if they speak English.

6. LONG-TERM PLANS

Sometimes living overseas with your company isn't viable long term. Sometimes it is a one-year plan, like my friend John, the environmental engineer. But in most cases, your company has a plan. Some of our early-on expat team members have been to three or four countries since we started this journey 14 years ago. They can decline the move, but most of the time the companies ask them just a year later and it is not always good if you keep telling your employer "no." So some of my friends simply take a stance of obedience in how God is leading them, and wherever they end up at work, they find ways to be missional. Others who have a strong sense of working with a certain people may need to find ways to be there, for example, by taking another job.

Possible Solutions

Talk with the employer on the front end and see if they

know how long the assignment would be. If nothing else, it may help you process the move. If you are in a situation where you want to stay where you are currently, then you may need to update a CV or résumé, attend networking events, and keep your eyes open. I have seen people find a way to switch jobs in order to stay. It is much harder if you want to stay with your company. In that case, you can always ask your superiors to stay. Many developed countries have what is called a Social Security agreement that allows you to work for a U.S. company paying into its Social Security system for only five years in a particular country.

CONCLUSION: NOT GOING ALONE

While writing this, I was talking to a friend of mine. We both had sons who were finishing up high school and preparing for college. His son always had a vision to go overseas and work among people in developing countries while taking the gospel there. He asked me about his son getting a Bible degree at a college. I told him, of course, that there is nothing inherently wrong with that, but I also suggested that he look at obtaining a civil engineering degree and find a job in the marketspace in that culture. He could also pursue some Bible classes to get a deeper theological background as needed. But he would have had his base: a solid degree for work. He called to tell me that his son is now enrolled at a very good engineering school and he took my advice. I cannot wait to see how God develops this young man's story.

How can we start encouraging students to take that view? For too long, they have heard from us as pastors and missionaries that if they are really serious about church or missions, then they need to throw themselves into it — prepare, get ordained, and go into full-time ministry. **We need people who have a calling to do that, but we also need to celebrate other pathways.**

All of this may seem complicated or daunting. I hope neither of these will deter you from what God may be up to in your life. As I mentioned earlier, I believe there is a basic assumption Jesus made when he gave us the Great Commission. He assumed that as disciples of his, as followers of the Way, we would naturally do what he did wherever we are living — whether that is in our own city or in a land far away.

Many years ago, when we first arrived on the field, I boarded a bus and headed to language school. The school was located in a different district. As we ascended the hill overlooking the large, urban area, I was struck by the sheer size of the city and how much work had to be done.

I was one of many who heard the Great Commission and sensed the Lord calling me overseas to make disciples. Being an overzealous, sometimes extremely-driven person, I had always been ready to take this on by myself. But for the first time, it really dawned on me that as I go, I am not going alone.

FOR THE FIRST TIME, IT REALLY DAWNED ON ME THAT AS I GO, I AM NOT GOING ALONE.

I have the promise of the Holy Spirit who will go with me as I go. As believers, we should also have the church to go along with us. I do not think we were ever meant to go on mission apart from the church. The church is a vital part of the Great Commission.

These days, I hear a lot about churches trying to be more evangelistic or missions-minded. Church leaders may create a new program or plan to attract people to the church in order to reach their communities. While the intention behind these programs and ideas may be right on target, I believe evangelism and missions can be much more personal. The special events and weekly meetings of a church are not designed to do the work that we as individual followers should do daily.

As I understand it, Jesus did not talk about how the church needs to have creative programs in order to reach people. Instead, he gave that job to each one of us as his followers.

Consider what Jesus says to the apostles, and ultimately to all his followers, in Acts 1:8:

- You will receive power.
- You will be my witnesses in Jerusalem, Judea, Samaria, and the uttermost parts of the earth.
- You will have the presence of Jesus in the Person of the Holy Spirit.

We are all "missionaries." We all have a missionary identity and a missionary responsibility to make disciples of all nations. Some people are called to live out this mission in another cultural context, but all of us are called to live it out wherever we are. That's what living missionally is all about.

It has been my hope with this book that you have seen

the perspectives of three vital relationships: the sending church, the marketplace worker, and the missionary team. All three of these relationships are important. As we go, I am convinced the best way forward in pursuing effective marketspace opportunities is through sending churches affirming this as a viable expression and pathway for missions. It is important for missionary teams who are on the ground to seek ways to provide community, accountability, and strategic direction for marketplace workers and not simply see them as second-class missionaries. We also need people who are willing to live, work, study, and even retire overseas, living intentionally and making disciples of all the nations.

We need each other!

About the Author

Larry E. McCrary co-founded The Upstream Collective in 2008. He has been involved in church planting for 25 years in both North America and Europe. He is a co-author of *Tradecraft for the Church on Mission*. He is married to Susan and they have two grown children who were raised overseas. Susan and Larry co-wrote the book *First 30 Daze: Practical Encouragement for Living Abroad Intentionally*. They both equip, coach, and care for marketspace workers who want to live intentionally in global settings.

Tradecraft: For the Church on Mission

Larry McCrary, Caleb Crider, Rodney Calfee, and Wade Stephens

The Western church world is abuzz with talk of being missional. Church leaders, conference speakers, and authors are weighing the merits of the attractional church movement of the past few decades, and where they find it lacking, prescribing changes in the way we need to approach our cultures with the Gospel. There has been a consensus shift among many churches, networks, and denominations to become more focused on mission. The result is a renewed interest in reaching the lost in our cities and around the world. The church, in many places in the Western world, is in fact returning to a biblical missional focus. Yet there is something still to be addressed in the process: the how. For centuries, God has called missionaries to cross cultures with the Gospel, and along the way, they have developed the necessary skill sets for a cultural translation of the good news. These skills need to be shared with the rest of the church in order to help them as well be effective missionaries. *Tradecraft for the Church on Mission* does exactly that. This book, in essence, pulls back the curtain on tools once accessible only to full-time Christian workers moving overseas, and offers them to anyone anywhere who desires to live missionally.

The Sending Church Defined
Zach Bradley

Purpose-driven church. Simple church. Organic church. Missional church. Deep church. Radical church. Transformational church. Total church. Sticky church. Tribal church. Mission-shaped church. Center church. Vertical church. Everyday church. Deliberate church. Gospel-centered church. Do we really need one more _____ church? "Yes!" say the collective of churches who consider themselves part of a growing movement called "sending church." It has proven itself as a term that is here to stay, but the meaning of it has been sadly mistaken. Many churches who call themselves sending churches are actually far from it. Some who are familiar with the term consider it just another missional trend. Others, upon first encounter think it speaks only to missiology. Sending church desperately needs clarity. That's precisely what this book is for.

It began with a gathering of sending churches who sought to answer the question, "What is a sending church?" They came up with a lengthy definition, and we then took almost a year to flesh out that definition one word at a time according to Scripture and scholarship. The goal was not just clarity, but to send a timely word to churches about reclaiming their birthright as the leaders in the Great Commission. After all, "A Sending church is a local community of Christ-followers who have made a covenant together to be prayerful, deliberate, and proactive in developing, commissioning, and sending their own members both locally and globally, often in partnership with other churches or agencies, and continuing to encourage, support, and advocate for them while making disciples cross-culturally."

First 30 Daze: Practical Encouragement for Living Abroad Intentionally

Larry and Susan McCrary

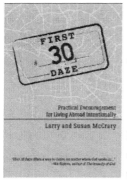

Being a part of a non-profit sector allows us to live in and travel to many cities in the United States, as well as in Europe. As followers of Jesus, wherever we live or travel, our goal is to live out our faith in a different culture. It does not matter if you are a full-time vocational Christian worker, an international company employee, a student studying abroad, or a person who simply wants to live and work in another country — the first 30 days matter! The sooner you can get out the door, learn the culture, meet people, build relationships, and discover what God has in store for you, the sooner you will feel at home and love your new environment. Thirty topics and Scripture verses are introduced, as well as practical ways to apply what you've learned each day through a simple but fun application assignment. You may want to use the book as an individual devotional, with your family, or with a group. Regardless, it is short and practical so that you have plenty of time to get out and enjoy your new home.

Order in bulk and get bulk pricing at:
http://theupstreamcollective.org/books

For more resources, training, and consulting to empower local churches on mission, visit:
http://theupstreamcollective.org